Spirit at Work

Jay A. Conger

and Associates

Spirit at Work

Discovering the Spirituality

in Leadership

Jossey-Bass Publishers • San Francisco

Substantial discounts on bulk quantities of Jossey-Bass books
are available to corporations, professional associations, and other
organizations. For details and discount information, contact the
special sales department at Jossey-Bass Inc., Publishers.
(415) 433-1740; Fax (415) 433-0499.

Manufactured in the United States of America. Nearly all Jossey-Bass
books and jackets are printed on recycled paper that contains at least
50 percent recycled waste, including 10 percent postconsumer waste.
Many of our materials are also printed with vegetable-based ink; during
the printing process these inks emit fewer volatile organic compounds
(VOCs) than petroleum-based ink. VOCs contribute to the formation
of smog.

Library of Congress Cataloging-in-Publication Data

Spirit at work : discovering the spirituality in leadership /
[contributions by] Jay A. Conger and associates. — 1st ed.
    p.   cm. — (The Jossey-Bass management series)
    Includes bibliographical references and index.
    ISBN 1-55542-639-5
    1. Leadership—Moral and ethical aspects. 2. Corporate culture.
3. Quality of work life. 4. Leadership—Religious aspects—
Christianity. 5. Spiritual life. I. Conger, Jay Alden.
II. Series.
HD57.7.S695   1994
658.4'092—dc20   94-5181
                                                       CIP

FIRST EDITION
HB Printing   10 9 8 7 6 5 4 3 2 1   *Code 9455*

The Jossey-Bass

Management Series

Contents

Preface

*T*his book is about the search for shared ground among leadership, the workplace, and spirituality, a relationship on which little has been said or written. For most of us, they are an unlikely trinity. In our stereotypes, spirituality and life in organizations are opposing forces—one taking us inward to ourselves, the other taking us outward to the world. The third side of the trinity, leadership, is another outward, activity-oriented force. How then can they ever connect? And why might we even wish for them to connect? These essential questions are at the heart of this volume.

Underlying the themes of the book is the premise that the workplace is today an essential arena of life for most of us—a place for connection and a place for contribution. It is also one of our most important sources of community. In contrast, some fifty years ago, many more communities existed to support us: the extended family, the civic community, and the church or temple. Yet if we think about these other communities, we find that most are in a sad state today. Many families are splintered by divorce, older children no longer live nearby, and grandparents, aunts, and uncles reside in faraway cities. Neighbors may not even know one another. Participation in the civic community has fallen prey to a fast-paced and individualistic society. Most of us do not have the time or interest to volunteer at the community center or sit on local education boards. And when it comes to the church or temple, few of us attend on a regular basis anymore. This, of course, brings the workplace and our immediate family to the forefront as our principal sources of community.

What has happened to those needs that the extended family and the civic and religious communities used to satisfy? Did they simply disappear? Or are the remnants of those communities still satisfying them? I, for one, suspect they are not. I wonder instead whether employees are not bringing to their work organizations, consciously or otherwise, some of those same needs for family, for community, and for spirituality. I also wonder whether some of the recent management books on leadership, on vision, on quality of work life, on empowerment, and on Japanese management practices do not have hidden within them a spiritual dimension.

Recently a friend mentioned the current interest in "servant leadership" being bantered around in books and articles about management. I could not help but think of the term's deeper associations with Christianity and the notion of being a "servant of the Lord" and serving humanity. I thought to myself, "Here is another example of spirituality in disguise!" Looking at the books on leaders' vision, we can see further connections to spirituality drawn by management thinkers. For example, Warren Bennis and Burt Nanus in their landmark book *Leaders* state that "by focusing attention on a vision, the leader operates on the *emotional and spiritual resources* of the organization, on its values, commitment, and aspirations."[1]

In both of these illustrations, we find management ideas that are attempts to heal the rift between an organization's needs for profitability and efficiency and its members' needs for growth and meaning. But what if we were to go a bit further and explore more explicitly the possibility of workplaces in which spirituality played an active role and the possibility that leadership was the enabling force? That very issue is what this book is all about. Each of the chapters is a visionary blueprint of how leadership, spirituality, and organizational life might meet on the same road and enrich our lives at work.

Overview of Contents

Chapter One is an introduction to the book's central themes. It sets the stage with a discussion of the ascendency of the workplace as a primary community for most of us. It also describes the equally rapid decline in our other communities, which is undermining our ability to satisfy deeply held needs for connection to a larger world and universe. It is around these two trends that the book seeks to find pathways to create workplace communities rooted in deeper and more spiritual connections. In addition, to provide a shared understanding of what we mean by spirituality, the introduction explores important basic questions such as "What is spirituality?" and "How is it different from religion?"

Chapter Two powerfully focuses our attention on the magnitude of the inner challenge that leaders must first face if they wish to lead from a more spiritually centered place. It highlights our tendency to understand leadership exclusively as the ability to manipulate the external world. In reality, as author Parker Palmer points out, there are critical internal dimensions. Drawing on the spiritual insight that we often project unresolved inner issues onto the world around us, this chapter defines a leader as someone who has the extraordinary power to project onto other people his or her darkness or light. It then explores five spiritual dilemmas that can make for pathological leadership—from the lack of a personal identity to the denial of death—and suggests various ways in which the spiritual traditions offer us help and health.

While Chapter Two helps us to understand the inner issues that must be faced if an individual is to lead with a spiritual presence, in Chapter Three, John Haughey provides us with a living example of one individual facing some of those issues and embodying the book's themes of leadership, spirituality, and organizational life: Vaclav Havel, the current president of the Czech republic. Living within a communist state devoid of a spiritual foundation, Havel sensed the emotional impact of spirituality's absence on the soul of his nation. Through personal integrity fostered by his own spirituality and his gift at articulating the human condition, Havel has been able to give new life to his society by encouraging authentic purposes of life rather than those guided by ideology and self-interest.

In Chapter Four Katherine Tyler Scott explains that to understand the possible connection between leadership and spirituality, we must first embrace a set of conflicting tensions and paradoxes. To do this requires full knowledge of our inner selves, of the relationship between our private and public lives, and of the formal organizational structures that we create. In all three of these areas, we must confront the difficulty and discomfort of dealing with opposites. For example, we often find rigid demarcations between our private and public lives, reserving the spiritual for the private and leadership for the public. Yet this very separation robs leaders of a view of the whole, resulting in actions guided by a rationality that may ultimately harm the spirit of an organization. Tyler Scott describes for readers an educational process that can help organizations face these opposing dimensions, embrace them, and manage the resulting ambiguity in ways that release and nurture the spirit within an organization. This chapter and the one that follows illustrate the book's themes from an organizational perspective and offer concrete ideas for educational approaches that can integrate our trinity.

In Chapter Five we continue our exploration into the educational processes that organizations can draw upon to tap spiritual resources. Authors Susan Wisely and Elizabeth Lynn contend that North American workplaces hold out rich resources to contemporary culture, because they serve their participants as essential arenas for connection to a larger world. At the Lilly Endowment, a private foundation based in Indianapolis, Indiana, Wisely and her colleagues have been working for the past decade to help nonprofit organizations cultivate these very resources. Through an extensive leadership education program for the community and for its own staff, the endowment has sought to create occasions that encourage people to make "spirited connections" with one another. These occasions are organized around a few age-old learning practices: for instance, participants are invited to engage in conversation and storytelling with one another, to study their common history, and to read and discuss books together. As simple as these practices may sound, they can contribute greatly to the spirit and mission of an organization, for they enable the members of the organization to discover their deeper relations to one another, relations extending beyond the tasks of the day or the psychological economy of the workplace, relations that are spiritual in nature. At the chapter's conclusion, Wisely and Lynn suggest ways in which organizational leaders can become spirited teachers, creating hospitable spaces where people can discover their connections to one another and to a larger creation.

In the next two chapters, we move from organizational processes to more personal processes that individuals can draw upon to enhance their spiritual side as they lead others. Brian McDermott in Chapter Six illustrates how the principles and methods of Ignatian spirituality can assist leaders seeking to deepen the influence of spirituality in their actions. By developing a contemplative attitude, we are able gradually to observe God's actions in the world by noticing our deepest desires and the orienting images that emerge from within us. From these vantage points, our leadership can be guided from more of a spiritual center.

Chapter Seven, written by Rabindra Kanungo and Manuel Mendonça, explores how leaders might effectively realize their spirituality in leading others by illustrating that spiritual experiences occur on three levels: the cognitive, the affective, and the behavioral. On the cognitive level, spirituality manifests itself in the realization that there exists a set of cardinal virtues and capital vices, and the spiritual goal of human beings is to live out the virtues and overcome the vices. By trusting in and depending on these virtues, we are able to experience the affective dimension of spirituality, which is a more blissful and emotionally rewarding experience of living. Finally, we live out these virtues and emotions in behavior that is both moral and altruistic. Such a set of experiences guides any leader who wishes to become more spiritually directed. Ultimately, leadership can then reach a stage where it seeks a continual self-transformation in the leader and in his or her followers. The authors describe how this process unfolds along the three dimensions.

Chapter Eight closes the book by examining the prospects for successful germination of the ideas presented here. We look at present-day attitudes toward spirituality in our society and how these may provide opportunities and obstacles for the realization of our trinity. An ancient folktale concludes our discussion by illustrating several of the book's essential themes, as well as highlighting critical issues that remain to be explored.

Acknowledgments

The unique character of this book is a reflection of its contributors, who were not only willing but excited to explore its relatively uncharted territory. Each of them endeavored to make this volume a very thoughtful and inspiring work. Their enthusiastic response to the project at its earliest stages encouraged me to pursue it even when faced with initial doubts about whether such a work would be feasible.

My friend Bob Burnside at the Center for Creative Leadership deserves a special thanks. Before the idea for this book ever materialized, Bob and I had encouraged each other to host a small conference on the topic. Its outcome led to the genesis for this book. Without Bob's fellowship, I am not sure I would have been inspired to undertake this effort. In addition, numerous conversations about spirituality and work with my friends and McGill colleagues Rabi Kanungo and Manuel Mendonça strengthened my view that a book addressing these issues was long overdue. Brian McDermott provided the wonderful title of *Spirit at Work*.

Finally, special thanks must go to my secretary, Pina Vicario, who I realize daily is my godsend—literally and figuratively. She has worked diligently with me on this project, helping me move beyond the many drafts to produce this unique volume.

Montreal, Quebec   Jay A. Conger
March 1994

Note

1. W. Bennis and B. Nanus, *Leaders* (New York: Harper & Row, 1985), 92.

The Authors

Jay A. Conger is associate professor of organizational behavior at the Faculty of Management, McGill University, Montreal. He received his B.A. degree (1974) in anthropology, with honors, from Dartmouth College, his M.B.A. degree (1977) from the University of Virginia, and his D.B.A. degree (1985) from the Harvard University Graduate School of Business Administration. He was recently invited to join the Harvard Business School as a visiting professor to assist in a major redesign of its curriculum around issues of leadership. He has also been a visiting professor at the European Institute of Business

Administration (INSEAD) in France, where he teaches executive programs. Conger consults worldwide in the areas of organizational change, leadership development, and management education and has been selected by *Business Week* as the "Pick of the Business School Professors" to teach leadership to executives worldwide. His fields of research interest include managing large-scale organizational change, executive leadership, empowerment, and the training and development of leaders and managers. He is particularly interested in the role that leaders play in entrepreneurship and change within their organizations and in motivating their workforce. His work on these subjects has been published in more than sixty articles, papers, and book chapters. His newest book, *Learning to Lead* (Jossey-Bass, 1992), examines how leadership ability can be developed in managers. Other recent books include *The Charismatic Leader* (Jossey-Bass, 1989) and *Charismatic Leadership* (Jossey-Bass, 1988, with Rabi N. Kanungo).

Father John Haughey, S.J., is a member of the Society of Jesus and a professor of religious ethics at Loyola University of Chicago. He is the editor of three volumes and the author of four books: *The Conspiracy of God: The Holy Spirit in Us* (1973); *Should Anyone Say Forever? On Making, Keeping and Breaking Commitments* (1975); *The Holy Use of Money: Personal Finances in the Light of Christian Faith* (1986); and *Converting 9 to 5: A Spirituality of Daily Work* (1989). Haughey was associate editor of the national journal of opinion

America from 1968 to 1974 and a member of the Woodstock Theological Center at Georgetown from its beginnings in 1974 to 1984. He has taught at Georgetown and Fordham Universities and has been a visiting professor at both Seton Hall University and the Weston School of Theology. In addition, he is a member of the Vatican Secretariat's team in dialogue with classical Pentecostalism. He is also a member of a number of boards: St. Joseph's University in Philadelphia; Bread for the World in Washington, D.C.; the National Center for the Laity; and the Catholic Health Association's theology and ethics commission.

Rabindra N. Kanungo is a professor of organizational behavior and holds the Faculty of Management Chair at McGill University, Montreal. He earned his B.A. degree (1953) with honors in economics and philosophy from Utkal University and his M.A. degree (1955) in psychology from Patna University. He received his Ph.D. degree in psychology from McGill University in 1962, and his work experience as a university professor, researcher, and consultant spans both East (India) and West (Canada and the United States). He has published widely in both the basic and applied areas of psychology and management. His publications include more than a hundred professional articles in such journals as *Experimental Psychology, Journal of Applied Psychology, Journal of Personality and Social Psychology, Academy of Management Review, California Management Review,* and *Psychological Bulletin.* He has written several books, including *Memory and Affect* (1975), *Biculturalism and Management* (1980), *Work Alienation* (1982), and *Compensation: Effective Reward Management* (1992). He is also author and co-editor of *Behavioral Issues in Management: The Canadian Context* (1977), *Management of Work and Personal Life* (1984), *Charismatic Leadership* (1988), and *Management in Developing Countries* (1990). For his contributions to psychology and management, Kanungo was elected a fellow of the Canadian Psychological Association and has won Commonwealth and Seagram Senior Faculty fellowships and Best Paper awards.

Elizabeth M. Lynn is associate program officer at the Spencer Foundation in Chicago, specializing in education research. She received her B.A. degree (1981) in American civilization from Brown University with honors and her M.A. (1986) and Ph.D. (1993) degrees in divinity from University of Chicago, with a special interest in the educational and spiritual uses of literature. For the past decade, she has served as a consultant to the evaluation program of Lilly Endowment. Lynn's previous publications include *Taken from the Ground: Leeds, Maine in the Twentieth Century* (1989) and *Variations on a Dream: Two Programs for Training Youth in Community Leadership and Service* (1985).

Reverend Brian O. McDermott, S.J., holds B.A. (1961) and M.A. (1964) degrees, both in philosophy, from Fordham University, an M.Div. degree (1968) from Woodstock

College in Maryland, an S.T.M. degree (1969) from Union Theological Seminary, and a Doctor of Theology degree (1973) from University of Nijmegen in the Netherlands. He has been a member of the faculty at Weston School of Theology in Cambridge, Massachusetts, since 1973 and has served as academic dean since 1991. McDermott was the religious superior of the Weston Jesuit Community in Cambridge. He entered the Society of Jesus (Jesuits) in 1956 and was ordained a Roman Catholic priest in 1968. His teaching and research interests include the significance of Jesus Christ and theological understandings of the human person. In addition, he is exploring the relationships between spirituality, particularly in the Ignatian tradition, and organizational life. In this connection, he is partnering with faculty involved in the leadership project at Harvard University's Kennedy School of Government. McDermott is the author of *What Are They Saying About the Grace of Christ?* (1984), and *Word Become Flesh: Dimensions of Christology* (1993), along with numerous articles in professional journals.

Manuel Mendonça teaches human resource management and managing organizational change in the Faculty of Management, McGill University, Montreal. He received his B.A. degree (1954) in economics and political science; his B.Com. degree (1955) in banking and M.A. degree (1960) in economics and sociology from St. Xavier's College, University of Bombay; and an M.B.A. (1978) in finance and organizational behavior from McGill

University, Montreal. He also holds a certificate in teaching from Concordia University, Montreal. His research interests are in the area of compensation and human resource management in the context of developing countries. He has co-authored two books, *Compensation: Effective Rewards Management* (1992) and *Introduction to Organizational Behavior* (1993). He is also a co-editor of *Work Motivation in Developing Countries* (in press). He has contributed to a number of refereed journals and books in his field, including articles in the *California Management Review, Psychology and Developing Societies,* and *Journal of Management Inquiry,* and chapters in *The Management of Organizations in Developing Countries* (1990) and *Organizational and Management Consultancy in Developing Countries* (1993). As a trainer, his recent activities include courses in group dynamics and people skills for leaders of religious congregations in northeastern India. Prior to his teaching and research activities, he held supervisory and management positions in the petrochemical and electrical industries in India. His interest in philosophy and theology and their implications for the practice of management was the outgrowth of participation in the monthlong Spiritual Exercises of St. Ignatius at St. Xavier's College, Bombay.

Parker Palmer received a B.A. degree (1961) in philosophy and sociology *cum laude* from Carleton College, where he was elected to Phi Beta Kappa and was awarded a Danforth Graduate Fellowship. After a year at

Union Seminary, he studied sociology at the University of California, Berkeley, where he received an M.A. degree (1965) and a Ph.D. (1970) with honors. Palmer is a writer, teacher, and activist who works independently on issues in education, community, spirituality, and social change. He also serves as senior associate of the American Association of Higher Education. His publications include ten poems, more than seventy essays, and four widely used books, including *The Promise of Paradox* (1980), *The Company of Strangers* (1981), *To Know As We Are Known* (1983), and *The Active Life* (1990). Dr. Palmer has also edited two collections: *The Recovery of Spirit in High Education* (1980) and *Caring for the Commonwealth* (1990). He is now writing a new book, *The Courage to Teach*.

Katherine Tyler Scott is a consultant and trainer to human service organizations, businesses, and churches, specializing in organizational and leadership development. She has a B.S. degree (1967) from Ball State University and an M.S.W. degree (1969) from Indiana University. Tyler Scott has more than twenty years of direct service and administrative and planning experience. She developed the Lilly Endowment Leadership Education Program and currently directs the Trustee Leadership Development Program, a national leadership education program for not-for-profit boards and staff. She has also developed leadership training resources for the National Association for Community Leadership and the National Episcopal Church. Tyler Scott is a graduate of the

Stanley K. Lacy Executive Leadership Program in Indianapolis. She has served on the Stanley K. Lacy alumni board, chaired several committees, and served terms of office as vice president and president of the alumni. She has been a member of the Indiana State Department of Mental Health Board, the Commission for Downtown, the board of the Indianapolis Chamber of Commerce, and the board of directors of the Greater Indianapolis Progress Committee. She is a founding member of the Indianapolis chapter of the Coalition of One Hundred Black Women and is currently a trustee of Park Tudor School and Arts Indiana, Inc. She is also a recipient of the Sagamore of the Wabash, the highest honor the governor of Indiana can bestow on a citizen, and was named the first recipient of the Indiana Youth Institute's Pathfinder Award in 1989 for her work in leadership education. Her co-authored book, *Stories from the Circle: Women's Leadership in Community,* was published in 1991. She is currently writing a book on trusteeship.

D. Susan Wisely is director of program evaluation for the Lilly Endowment. She received both her A.B. degree (1968), with high distinction and honors, and her M.A. degree (1969) in sociology from Indiana University. In her current position, she works with foundation officers and consultants to plan and implement evaluation studies to inform the foundation's future work. She joined the staff of the endowment twenty years ago after teaching social psychology at Indiana University and serving as planning and research director for a federally funded employment program. During her tenure at the Lilly Endowment, Wisely has had major responsibility for grant programs benefiting youth and Native Americans. In 1983, the endowment established two foundationwide committees: the leadership education committee and the youth committee. Wisely served as the first convenor of the youth committee and has been a member of the leadership education committee since its formation. As an extension of her valuation responsibilities, she devotes attention to the foundation's continuing education and planning efforts. She is also adviser to the Council on Foundations on evaluation issues.

Spirit at Work

1

Introduction
Our Search for Spiritual Community

Jay A. Conger

*F*or many of us, the work-place has become our primary source of community. It is where we spend the majority of our time. It is where many of our friendships and relationships take place. It is where we seek a good deal of our challenges in life. It is where we contribute to our society.

Yet it is also here that our loyalty is often the weakest. It is here that we are often inadequately challenged and underutilized. It is here that we find it difficult to see connections between our immediate work and a contribution to society. It is here that words like *empower-*

ment are promoted because such feelings are so often absent. These are the contradictions of our workplace today.

The desire to change this situation—to create a workplace that is humane, that provides community, that promotes a sense of higher purpose—has been gaining momentum since the days of Harvard psychologist Abraham Maslow and management thinker Douglas MacGregor. Yet the search has never been so pronounced as it is today, when the workplace has become a central community for so many. Its increased importance reflects the ebb of other communities that once served our needs for growth and connection. The extended family has been splintered by the jet age and by divorce rates. Churches and temples, which long served as important places for connection, have seriously diminished in their impact as their rituals and traditions have drifted from everyday lives. The civic community that once nourished our needs for contribution has fallen prey to cynicism and apathy and to lives that are too busy.

Within a matter of a few decades, the ability of these other communities to provide satisfying links to others and to a greater good has lessened dramatically. Yet our needs and longings for spirituality, for community, and for contribution have not diminished. Instead they have, for most of us, simply slid into neglect. This neglect is in turn creating a growing hunger. While new communities such as support groups for single parents or for children of alcoholics or even for dating have appeared, they will probably not be sufficient. Instead our workplace and immediate family surroundings are likely to remain the two communities where we will continue to spend the majority of our time, and therefore the communities where we must somehow discover a new means to nourish ourselves and our souls.

These two fundamental changes—the ascendency of the workplace as a primary community and our growing inability to satisfy needs for connection and contribution—are the impetus for this book.

I am a baby-boomer. Like many people my age, I have felt within my own self a rumbling of the needs I have just been describing. Among the most important of these rumblings is a sense that my spiritual side has been dormant for too long. It is an ironic feeling, since most of my childhood Sundays were spent at church. I still have vivid memories of rising from the church pew to say, "Our father who art in Heaven, hallowed be thy name." Memories of singing a favorite hymn at the top of my voice. Memories of communions, baptisms, weddings that took place in the red brick church that my parents still attend to this day.

But these rituals had limited meaning for me then. Something was missing. There was a certain mundaneness—the rituals were often motions rather than emotions. And even as a child I could see the inconsistencies between what was preached and what was practiced.

When I reached college, the Beatles were introducing musician Ravi Shankar and the Indian guru Maharishi to the Western world. The former Harvard professor

Richard Alpert became Ram Dass and simultaneously a spiritual folk hero. He had dropped out of Harvard, traveled to India, and turned on to meditation. His books and ideas would excite many of us into becoming aficionados of Eastern religions. Other new ideas about spirituality would pour in from books by Herman Hesse and Alan Watts and from the Indian tales of the Upanishads and the *Bhagavadgita*. Suddenly, spirituality took on an exotic and mysterious air. It was exciting—especially compared to those long Sunday sermons. Spirituality had now become like an adventure-filled travel book. But similar to pictures in a travel book, these ideas were mostly imaginations and abstractions. So by age twenty, I had imagined spiritual experiences far more than I had ever *experienced* them.

Then came the summer after my sophomore year in college. I had been invited to work in Turkey as an archaeologist, and there for the first time I had an emotional taste of a spiritual side. My job was to help unearth an ancient theater in the Greek and Roman city of Aphrodisias. Each evening, when the heat of the day had calmed, I would take an evening stroll. As the skyline turned to warm streaks of red and purple, I would wander among the temple ruins, down the Roman streets, and into the ancient stadium. A light, warm wind would often pass through the stadium at evening time, whistling as it moved through. My imagination would begin to play, and soon the sound of the wind would transform itself into Roman crowds jumping up from their seats and cheering for their teams in contests. In my mind's eye, I could imagine the thousands of people who had lived on before me.

After the stadium I would pass by a magnificent temple devoted to Aphrodite, whose remaining columns would turn a pastel rouge as the sunset became their backdrop. There I could feel even more profoundly the mystery of a ruined city. The combination of those pockmarked shafts of marble reaching upward, the tumble of fallen stones all around, and the serenity of evening time created a feeling of magic. It was also a feeling of my mortality. After all, I knew that before me lay two thousand years of human life. Mine was to be only a moment in that scheme. Yet somehow the beauty and grandeur of the place reassured me. I could feel at some very deep place that a remarkable force existed beyond me and beyond humanity, a God who had somehow put all of this together. This was a force both eternal and creative. I can remember wondering what the world would be like if we had such moments daily.

That summer would be the first of several deeply personal experiences where I could emotionally sense a connection to a power greater than myself and others. It would spark my curiosity, and I would begin to explore my own spirituality through visits to meditation retreats, to monasteries from Vermont to India, to churches of different faiths, to lectures, and to the spirituality sections of bookstores.

In recent years, however, something has happened to this spiritual side. Like many of my friends, I have found it difficult to find a local religious community that truly nourishes my soul on a weekly basis. My career and personal life now take far more of my time than ever before. So today, the workplace and the home have become my principal communities. The home can nourish my spirit through intimacy, but my workplace is far less effective. My daily work—teaching, researching, and working with clients—sustains a portion of my spirituality, but more often it feels like a separate activity. A sense of connection to a larger universe and to a community that seeks the best for one another and for the planet is largely missing from the workplace that I now know.

In my growing frustration over this gap between my work life and my spiritual life, I decided to organize in 1992 a small gathering of people interested in management and spirituality to begin wrestling with possible intersections of these two seemingly disparate fields. I would add a third topic to the mix—leadership. My reasoning at the time was quite straightforward. After studying leadership for a decade, I had come to believe that leaders are often the strongest force in shaping the orientation of their organizations. If any single catalyst in an organization is likely to bring about a spiritual presence into the workplace, it is a leader. These notions would form the original focus of the conference. I also had a personal hope for this conference. I wished it to be the first of many personal initiatives to integrate a spiritual dimension into my own work.

With my friend and co-organizer Bob Burnside from the Center for Creative Leadership, I hoped to find "like souls"—mostly management professors—who shared our interests. Almost immediately we learned something quite fascinating. We had originally estimated that we might find a dozen or so interested colleagues. But as we began to call people, one after another of our contacts informed us of three or four other interested individuals. It was like a secret society where suddenly you discover that half of your acquaintances are members. Few of us had ever talked publicly about these issues; we were like warm coals with our fires hidden within.

From that conference, I would gain several important insights. I would learn that many of us in my field of management, while deeply curious about spirituality in the workplace, are reluctant to speak to these issues publicly. Unlike rabbis, priests, and ministers, we are not in the profession of serving others in a spiritual capacity, especially on a daily basis. Therefore we feel we lack a certain expertise to speak with any authority.

Second, we are anxious about how others might perceive us, or rather misperceive us; we fear that if we speak to these issues we will be seen as evangelists or missionaries rather than as simply curious, spiritually inclined individuals. This fear keeps us from being more public about our interest and perhaps from exploring it more concretely.

Finally, we feel a deep respect for the sacredness of spirituality. Having seen too many management ideas turned into money-generating techniques, we fear the same misfortune will befall a spiritual exploration into the world of work. Someone out there will turn spirituality into a $400-a-day workshop on improving employee morale. And sadly, there is a good probability that this could happen.

Yet my feeling has been that we could not allow these concerns to stop us from making a responsible attempt to explore these issues. I have been sensing over the last few years a not-so-subtle groundswell of interest by managers, human resources experts, management professors, clergy, and trainers in the possibility of a more spiritual-centered workplace. Though interest and curiosity are rapidly growing, few if any attempts have been made to address the topic in a meaningful way. If we made such an attempt with a spirit of humbleness and care, I sensed that we could at least spark some ideas, some insights, some possibilities and perhaps guard to some extent against the exploitation of spirituality. It is from this belief that the book that you are reading took form.

In my search for contributors to this volume, I realized that individuals who stood on the cusp between organizational life and spirituality were in the best position to help us explore these issues. They felt the most comfortable in talking about spirituality, leadership, and organizational life. Most of us in the field of management faced too many of the dilemmas I have just been describing to feel at ease speaking on these issues in depth. So in this book you will see few management professors and instead more foundation directors, theologians, and nonprofit educators who deal directly with organizational life in their work. All of them have had an ongoing interest in making the workplace a more spiritual space, a place of connection and growth for the soul.

That is how and why this book came about. As we begin our journey, perhaps it would be useful to address some basic questions that are likely to be on your mind: What is spirituality? How is it different from religion? Why is spirituality so important to our lives in the first place? And why the current interest in spirituality and the workplace?

Spirituality and Religion: Is There a Difference?

Many of us associate the word *spiritual* with images of saints or monks like St. Augustine or Thomas Merton. They embody a sense of being removed from the material world, of an ascetic lifestyle, of inward reflection, of detachment. Yet in a recent study on spirituality, Wade Clark Roof, a religion professor at the University of California, Santa Barbara, found a far different interpretation of spirituality among middle-aged Americans: "In its truest sense, spirituality gives expression to the being that is in us; it has to do with feelings, with the power that comes from within, with knowing our deepest selves and what is sacred to us, with, as Matthew Fox says, 'heart-knowledge.'"[1]

In contrast to our stereotypes, then, spirituality is very much of this world. For many of us it is grounded in living feelings. Presumably most of us have access to such feelings though quite probably not on command. When we *feel* the sacredness of a moment, of an experience, of a person, of the world, we are having a spiritual experience of some sort. Many times, these feelings are rooted in a sense of transcendence in its broadest interpretation. Turning to the dictionary, we find the following definitions for the word *transcendental:* "exceeding usual limits" and "extending or lying beyond the limits of ordinary experience."[2] If we apply these interpretations to spirituality, we could say that it is experienced in those moments when we literally transcend ourselves (exceed the usual limits of our self-interest), such as in selfless love or social justice, or when we are able to extend our vision and feelings beyond the ordinary to discern an extraordinary, godly presence in our lives and universe.

I would add, however, a word of caution here. Since spiritual experiences stem from feelings, they are highly subjective. One person's spiritual experiences may be quite different from another's. Ancient ruins in Turkey may produce a spiritual experience for one person but not necessarily for another. My own attempt at defining spirituality, while a helpful start, is also potentially limiting. There may be other manifestations depending on the individual and that person's background. In addition, my Christian upbringing influences my own sense of spirituality: I see or feel *a* God in the universe. A Hindu might feel the presence and character of Vishnu or Shiva instead.

To illustrate this variety in spiritual experiences, let

10

---

us look at two different examples from Roof's research. Linda, a born-again Christian living in Ohio, feels her spiritual experience as

> a journey in which one must constantly work at strengthening faith through prayer and Bible study, or as born-again Christians say, "walking with the Lord," or "walking the Christian walk." This walk involves submitting one's life to Christ and cultivating Christ-like virtues, such as love, humility, patience, and forgiveness. In addition, there are the biblical injunctions to refrain from the works of the flesh, such as uncleanness, adultery, idolatry, drunkenness, and the like. At the center of this worldview is an unfaltering belief that Jesus Christ was sent by God to save the world and that salvation is possible only through him.[3]

Contrast this with the comments of a neurologist who is a Jewish agnostic married to a Seventh-Day Adventist.

> I'm certainly not religious, in the sense that I don't believe in God and I don't subscribe to standard religious doctrine; but I think I'm spiritual, in the sense that I have a very deep sense of world realities. I don't know where they come from. . . . [My wife] says they come from God, of course, from Judeo-Christian tradition, which may be true, but I don't know . . . but I feel extremely strong about the importance of right actions for others, being

fair to others. A lot of these things came out of the civil rights movement. I have very strong feelings about that. I get extremely upset or angry when I see evidence of injustice or prejudice. And that to me, that's part of being spiritual. Another part of being spiritual to me is sort of this sense of reverence about the world, which I think religious people attribute to God or their relationship to God; for me, it's much more abstract. And again I'm not sure where it comes from, I think I'm probably more sensitive than most people, at least most people I'm in contact with, to reap the beauty of the world and history and life and how moving it is to wake up in the morning and see the flowers coming up and the clouds in the sky.[4]

The differences between the two are, of course, quite striking, demonstrating once again that spirituality is a highly personal experience. Yet there are certain themes that cut across the variety of experiences: a selfless sense of love and compassion for others, respect and concern for well-being and life, and reverence for the universe and its creation.

Historically, religion has been intertwined with these feelings by creating situations that can foster spiritual experiences for us. Through the grandeur of a cathedral or the meditative experience of a written prayer or the lyrics of a moving hymn, formal religion can encourage spiritual experiences. It may even define the feelings for us. But spirituality and religion are not necessarily one and the same.

For example, while conducting his research, Roof asked people whether they perceived a difference between being "spiritual" and being "religious." The consistent response was yes, although agreement on the essential differences was less clear. There was also widespread agreement that the two had become disconnected from each other in today's world. What emerged was that for many individuals, the term *religious* had an institutional connotation. It meant practicing rituals, adhering to dogma, and attending services. Spirituality, as we have been discussing it, had more to do with life's deeper motivations and an emotional connection to God. As one Roman Catholic respondent in the survey commented: "To me religion is practicing . . . going to church . . . receiving Communion. Spiritual to me is just being in touch with your higher power."[5]

Interestingly, we are at one of those junctures in Western history where the two have been uncoupling. The more the institutional trappings and philosophy of a religion become disjointed from the everyday needs of its followers, the more likely a schism is approaching. People then turn away from their religious institution as their sole source of spiritual sustenance and begin to seek other sources within themselves or in new communities. Roof's comments on North American baby-boomers then begin to apply: "If religious institutions . . . lack vitality and seem removed from their everyday lives, boomers are inclined to judge them to be empty and irrelevant. Worse still, just going through the motions of religious involvement can easily smack of hypocrisy to a generation that has felt estranged from social institutions and insists upon authenticity and credibility as prerequisites for commitment."[6]

It is not so surprising that one of the top-selling books today is Thomas Moore's *Care of the Soul,* which illustrates how we can nourish our spirit in the small everyday events of life.[7] On best-seller lists for more than *five hundred* weeks is Scott Peck's *The Road Less Traveled,* which highlights how psychotherapy may help us connect to our spirituality.[8] Both are guides for finding spirituality beyond the bonds of religious institutions.

As the direct impact of religion on our lives lessens, many of us are turning to other arenas or means whereby we can nourish our spirituality. Though it borrows from religion, this book itself is a reflection of that search.

Why Is Spirituality So Important to Us?

I cannot pretend to be any kind of expert when it comes to answering the question of spirituality's role in our lives. But it seems to me that people yearn for spirituality for several fundamental reasons.

I believe that at some deep level all of us sense the tremendous uncertainty connected with life. With age, we become acutely aware of the greatest uncertainty: what lies beyond the moment of death? Spirituality for many of us brings solace and hope that there is more beyond our lives here on earth. That there is a master plan, not random chaos. That we will not simply disintegrate into nothingness but continue on in some form.

Life is full of pain. Few of us have been spared pain, whether it be physical or emotional or both. In our suffering, we need to know that there is hope, that there is some force larger than us that we can turn to, that we can ultimately trust in. Some of us need to feel as well that there is a reason for suffering, that it has to do with our own growth and perhaps a divine plan. I often feel that suffering brings me closer to God. In those moments, I lose my sense that I am in control, I lose my sense of my own mastery. I must turn to others and to God for love, support, and hope. Because of suffering, I must open myself to other powers.

Most of us have a wellspring of selfless love within, and spirituality is very much connected to this. Whether it is in caring for a baby, showing compassion for others, acting altruistically, or promoting social justice, this force yearns for expression.

Finally, I think that many of us see and feel a certain grandeur and mystery to the world and a certain connection among all humanity. In special moments, I will find myself standing in profound awe of life and our interconnections, and in those moments I feel very deeply my belief in a God who is a miraculous creator.

These are just some of the forces that motivate us spiritually. With the disintegration of many of our support communities, the growing disappointment with the imagined rewards of materialism, and the enormous psychological suffering and stress that so many of us experience, these are ripe times for spirituality—not a spirituality confined narrowly to certain institutions or rituals or traditions but a spirituality rooted in relationships and in everyday experiences.

Spirituality and the Study of Management

Our workplace is now one of our most important communities. Yet it is perhaps the one least equipped to be a real *community*. In the past, the roles of communities were well defined, and work was the place to earn a living, not to experience spirituality or family or civic contribution. Its very nature makes rocky soil for many of the traditional approaches to spirituality such as prayer or meditation or religious ideals. There is the everyday hustle-bustle, the race to meet deadlines, the mundane administrative chores, the poor bosses, the demoralized subordinates, the bureaucracy, the lack of recognition, the strong presence of materialism, and the pull of personal ambition. All these forces plus dozens of others make it hard to feel part of a deeply supportive community that is contributing to a larger and more interconnected world.

During the last several decades, my field of management—organizational behavior—has concerned itself directly with improving the quality of work life, with enhancing the sense of community in organizations. As teachers and consultants, we have proposed systems of work that are more challenging, rewards that are more than just money, teamwork that is more than just meetings, change processes that are more humane in their impact. We have written and taught about empowerment and vision and motivation and transformational leadership. We have consulted with managers on how to apply these processes. And while our efforts have raised the consciousness among some organizations, there is a sense that much remains to be done. Many of the original ideas and practices, for example, have become mechanical processes that managers implement one day and lose heart with the next day. The right motions may be made, but the right emotions and mindsets are still missing.

Some of us are coming to an interest in spirituality as a more profound solution. For spirituality, more powerfully than most other human forces, lifts us beyond ourselves and our narrow self-interests. When not misused, it is the most humane of forces. It helps us to see our deeper connections to one another and to the world beyond ourselves. Others of us simply have strong spiritual yearnings that are now seeking expression in a new arena—our work.

In either case, unlike any of our previous efforts, spirituality will not lend itself to management techniques. Rather, it presents the most complex challenge we could face in attempting to enhance workplace life, but also potentially the most rewarding.

With these thoughts in mind, we can begin our journey. We start in the next chapter with a look at the profound inner task that awaits readers wishing to be guided from a spiritual center.

Notes

1. W. C. Roof, *A Generation of Seekers: The Spiritual Journeys of the Baby Boom Generation* (San Francisco: HarperCollins, 1993), 64.
2. *Webster's New Collegiate Dictionary* (Springfield, Mass.: G & C Merriam, 1976).
3. Roof, *Generation,* 92.
4. Roof, *Generation,* 77–78.
5. Roof, *Generation,* 76–77.
6. Roof, *Generation,* 78.
7. T. Moore, *Care of the Soul* (San Francisco: HarperCollins, 1993).
8. S. Peck, *The Road Less Traveled* (New York: Touchstone, 1978).

2

Leading from Within
Out of the Shadow,
into the Light[1]

Parker J. Palmer

*I*n the last decade or two, we have done a lot of moaning about the lack of moral, humane, and visionary leadership in the public arena. But today, if we have eyes to see, we can look around the world and find those moral, visionary, humane leaders. We can find them in South Africa, we can find them in Latin America, and we can find them in eastern Europe.

I want to begin these reflections with the words of one of those people, someone whose credentials for leadership are far more authentic than mine. Vaclav

19

Havel (playwright, dissident, prisoner, and then president of Czechoslovakia) addressed the U.S. Congress in early 1990. It was surely one of the most remarkable speeches ever delivered on the floor of our national legislative body.

> As long as people are people, democracy, in the full sense of the word, will always be no more than an ideal. In this sense, you too are merely approaching democracy uninterruptedly for more than 200 years, and your journey toward the horizon has never been disrupted by a totalitarian system.
>
> The communist type of totalitarian system has left both our nations, Czechs and Slovaks, as it has all the nations of the Soviet Union and the other countries the Soviet Union subjugated in its time, a legacy of countless dead, an infinite spectrum of human suffering, profound economic decline, and, above all, enormous human humiliation. It has brought us horrors that fortunately you have not known. [I think we Americans should confess that some in our country *have* known such horrors.— P.J.P.]
>
> It has given us something positive, a special capacity to look from time to time somewhat further than someone who has not undergone this bitter experience. A person who cannot move and lead a somewhat normal life because he is pinned under a boulder has more time to think about his hopes than someone who is not trapped that way.

20

What I'm trying to say is this: We must all learn many things from you, from how to educate our offspring, how to elect our representatives, all the way to how to organize our economic life so that it will lead to prosperity and not to poverty. But it doesn't have to be merely assistance from the well-educated, powerful and wealthy to someone who has nothing and therefore has nothing to offer in return.

We too can offer something to you: Our experience and the knowledge that has come from it. The specific experience I'm talking about has given me one certainty: Consciousness precedes being, and not the other way around, as the Marxists claim. For this reason, the salvation of this human world lies nowhere else than in the human heart, in the human power to reflect, in human meekness and in human responsibility. Without a global revolution in the sphere of human consciousness, nothing will change for the better in the sphere of our beings as humans, and the catastrophe toward which this world is headed—be it ecological, social, demographic or a general breakdown of civilization—will be unavoidable.[2]

I doubt there has ever been, from a more remarkable source, a stronger affirmation of the link between spirituality and leadership than Havel's words, "consciousness precedes being" and "the salvation of the world lies in the human heart." He points us toward the heart of the matter—the formation of the human heart, the reformation of the human heart, and the rescuing of the human heart from all its deformations.

Material realities, he tells us, are not the fundamental factor in the movement of history. Consciousness is. Human awareness is. Thought is. Spirit is. Those are the deep sources of freedom and power with which oppressed people historically have been able to move immense boulders and create remarkable change.

But let me say something that Vaclav Havel was too polite to say: It is not only the Marxists who have believed that matter is more powerful than consciousness. It is not only the Marxists who have believed that economics is more fundamental than spirit. It is not only the Marxists who have believed that the flow of cash creates more reality than does the flow of ideas. We capitalists have believed these things too, and Havel was simply too nice to say it. But we can say it to ourselves. We can remind ourselves that in our own system of thought we have a long and crippling legacy of believing in the power of the external world much more deeply than we believe in the power of the internal world.

How many times have you heard or said, "Those are good ideas, inspiring notions, but the *reality* is . . ."? How many times have you heard people trying to limit our creativity by treating institutional realities as absolute constraints on what we are able to do? How many times have you worked in systems based on the belief that the only changes that really matter are the ones that you can count or measure or tally up externally? This is not just a Marxist problem. This is a human problem, at least in our twentieth-century, technological society.

We are not victims of that society, we are its co-creators. The great insight of our spiritual traditions is that external reality does not impinge upon us as a prison or as an ultimate constraint. Instead we *co-create* that reality. We live in and through a complex interaction of spirit and matter, a complex interaction of what is inside of us and what is "out there." The wisdom of our spiritual traditions is not to deny the reality of the outer world, but to help us understand that we create the world, in part, by projecting our spirit on it—for better or worse.

Vaclav Havel has said some hard things to his own people about how they conspired in the domination of a tyrannical communist system through their own passivity. We too are responsible for the existence of tyrannical conditions, of external constraints that crush our spirits, because we too co-create reality through the projection of our internal limitations. Our complicity in world-making is a source of awesome and sometimes painful responsibility and at the same time a source of profound hope for change.

The great spiritual traditions are not primarily about values and ethics, not primarily about doing right or living well. The spiritual traditions are primarily about *reality.* The spiritual traditions all strive to penetrate the illusions of the external world and to name its underlying truth—what it is, how it emerges, and how we relate to it.

In my own tradition, I have been rereading some of Jesus's sayings that I was taught as ethical exhortations, as guides to what we *ought* to do: "The person who seeks life will lose it; but the person who is willing to lose life will find it." But that is not an ethical exhortation. It is not an "ought" statement. It is simply a description of what *is*! Time and again, things Jesus said that we take as ethical pronouncements are simply his statements of what is real. That is the nature of great spiritual teaching.

The insight that I want to draw from the spiritual traditions, and from Havel, may be best summarized in a word from depth psychology: *projection.* We share responsibility for creating the external world by projecting either a spirit of light or a spirit of shadow on that which is other than us. We project either a spirit of hope or a spirit of despair, either an inner confidence in wholeness and integration or an inner terror about life being diseased and ultimately terminal. We have a choice about what we are going to project, and in that choice we help create the world that is. Consciousness precedes being, and consciousness can help deform, or reform, our world.

Leaders Have a Shadow Side

What does all of this have to do with leadership and with the relation of leadership to spirituality? Here is a quick definition of a leader: A leader is a person who has an unusual degree of power to project on other people his or her shadow, or his or her light. A leader is a person who has an unusual degree of power to create the conditions under which other people must live and move and have their being, conditions that can either be as illuminating as heaven or as shadowy as hell. A leader must take special responsibility for what's going on inside his or her own self, inside his or her consciousness, lest the act of leadership create more harm than good.

I want to look here at the shadow side of leadership. Many books on leadership seem to be about the power of positive thinking. I fear they feed a common delusion among leaders that their efforts are always well intended, their power always benign. I suggest that the challenge is to examine our consciousness for those ways in which we leaders may project more shadow than light.

By *leaders,* I do not mean simply the heads of nation-states. I am talking, for example, about a classroom teacher who has the power to create the conditions under which young people must spend half of their waking hours, five days a week, week in and week out. We know that there are classrooms where the leader projects a welcoming light under which new growth flourishes. But we also know of classrooms where the leader casts an ominous shadow under which nothing can grow. I am talking also about a parent who can generate the same effects in a family, about a clergyperson who can create a congregation that lurks in the leader's shadow or thrives in his or her light. I am talking about the CEO of a corporation who faces the same choice every day but who often does not even know that a choice is being made, let alone know how to reflect upon the process.

The problem is that people rise to leadership in our society by a tendency toward extroversion, which too often means ignoring what is going on inside themselves. Leaders rise to power by operating very competently and effectively in the external world, sometimes at the cost of internal awareness. Leaders, in the very way they become leaders, tend to screen out the inner consciousness that Vaclav Havel is calling us to attend to. I have met too many leaders whose confidence in the external world is so high that they regard the inner life as illusory, a waste of time, a magical fantasy trip into a region that does not even exist. But the link Havel makes between consciousness and reality, between leadership and spirituality, calls us to reexamine that common denial of the inner life.

I think leaders often feed themselves on the power of positive thinking because their jobs are hard. They face many external discouragements and they get little affirmation. Thus they feel a need to psych themselves up even if it means ignoring the inner shadow. Of course, leaders are supported in this by an American culture that wants to externalize everything, that wants (just as much as Marx ever did) to see the good life more as a matter of outer arrangements than of inner well-being.

I have looked at some training programs for leaders, and I am discouraged by how often they focus on the development of skills to manipulate the external world rather than the skills necessary to go within and make the spiritual journey. I find that discouraging because it feeds a dangerous syndrome among leaders who already tend to deny their inner world.

The Nature of Spirituality

Spirituality, like leadership, is a very hard concept to pin down. These are probably two of the vaguest words you can find in our language, and when you put them together you get something even more vague.

So let me share a remarkably concrete quote from Annie Dillard's wonderfully titled book, *Teaching a Stone to Talk*. Never have I read a more evocative description of the inner journey:

> In the deeps are the violence and terror of which psychology has warned us. But if you ride these monsters down, if you drop with them farther over the world's rim, you find what our sciences cannot locate or name, the substrate, the ocean or matrix or ether which buoys the rest, which gives goodness its power for good, and evil its power for evil, the unified field: our complex and inexplicable caring for each other, and for our life together here. This is given. It is not learned.[3]

Annie Dillard is saying several things that are very important for a spirituality of leadership. She is saying, first of all, that the spiritual journey moves inward and downward, not outward and upward toward abstraction. It moves downward toward the hardest concrete

realities of our lives—a reversal of what we traditionally have understood spirituality to be.

Why must we go in and down? Because as we do
so, we will meet the violence and terror that we carry
within ourselves. If we do not confront these things inwardly, we will project them outward onto other people. When we have not understood that the enemy is
within ourselves, we will find a thousand ways of making someone "out there" into the enemy—people of a
different race, a different gender, a different sexual orientation. We will deal with our fears by killing the enemy,
when what we really fear is the shadow within ourselves.

Annie Dillard is saying we have to go down and
in, and on the way we will meet our own monsters. But
if we ride those monsters all the way down, we find the
most precious thing of all: "the unified field, our complex and inexplicable caring for each other," the community we have underneath our brokenness—which,
Dillard says, is given, not learned. Great leadership
comes from people who have made that downward
journey through violence and terror, who have touched
the deep place where we are in community with each
other, and who can help take the rest of us to that place.
That is what great leadership is all about.

That is also what Vaclav Havel is talking about, because the downward journey is what you take when you
are under a stone for forty years. That is what you have
a chance to do when you are a victim of oppression.
Is it not remarkable that Nelson Mandela used decades

in prison to prepare himself for leadership rather than for despair? Under the most destructive circumstances, he went down, he went in, he dealt with the violence and terror, and he emerged as a leader able to take people toward "our complex and inexplicable caring for each other." It seems to me that this is a powerful image for the spiritual journey, the journey that leaders must take if Havel and Dillard are right.

Now the question is, why would anybody want to take such a difficult and dangerous journey? Everything in us cries out against it. That is why we externalize everything—it is far easier to deal with the external world. It is easier to spend your life manipulating an institution than dealing with your own soul. We make institutions sound complicated and hard and rigorous, but they are simplicity itself compared with our inner labyrinths!

Let me tell you a little parable about why one might want to take the inner journey, a parable from my own life. About ten years ago, when I was in my early forties, I decided to go on that amazing program called Outward Bound. I was in the midst of a midlife crisis, and I thought Outward Bound might be a useful challenge.

I elected to spend ten days at a place called Hurricane Island. I should have known from the name what was in store for me. Next time I will choose the program at Pleasant Valley or Happy Gardens! It was a week of sheer terror. It was also a week of amazing growth and great teaching and a deep sense of community, the likes of which I have seldom experienced.

In the middle of that Outward Bound course I faced the challenge that I had most feared. The leaders backed me up to the edge of a cliff 110 feet above solid ground. They tied a frayed and very thin rope to my waist, and told me to back down that cliff.

So I said, "Well, what do I do?"

The instructor, in typical Outward Bound fashion, said, "Just *go!*"

So I went, and slammed down onto a small ledge, with considerable force.

The instructor looked down at me. "I don't think you quite have it yet."

"Right. *Now* what do I do?"

"The only way to do this is to lean back as far as you can. You have to get your feet at right angles to the rock face so you'll have your full weight on them."

Of course I *knew* that he was wrong. I knew that the trick was to hug the mountain, to stay as close to the rock face as I could. So I tried it again, and *BOOM!* I hit the next ledge, hard.

"You still don't have it," the instructor said.

And I said, "Well, what do I do?"

And he said, "Lean way back and take the next step."

The next step was a very big one, but I took it. Wonder of wonders, I began to get the knack. I leaned back, and sure enough, I was moving down the rock face, eyes on the heavens, making tiny, tiny, tiny movements with my feet but gaining confidence with every step.

When I got about halfway down, a second instructor called up from below. "Parker," she said, "I think you better stop and look at what's happening beneath your feet."

Very slowly I lowered my eyes, and there beneath my feet a large hole was opening up in the rock.

To get around the hole, I was going to have to change directions. I froze, completely paralyzed in sheer terror.

The second instructor let me hang there for what seemed like a very long time, and finally she shouted up, "Parker, is anything wrong?"

To this day, I do not know where these words came from, though I have twelve witnesses that I spoke them. But in a high, squeaky voice I said, "I don't want to talk about it."

"Then I think it's time you learned the motto of the Outward Bound School."

"Oh, great," I thought. "I'm about to die, and she's giving me a motto!"

But then she yelled up to me words that I will never forget, words that have been genuinely empowering for me ever since. "The motto of the Outward Bound Hurricane Island School is, 'If you can't get out of it, get into it!'"

I have believed in the idea of "the word became flesh" for a long time, but I had never had a real experience of it. But those words seemed so profoundly true to me at that existential moment that they entered my body, bypassed my mind, and animated my legs and feet. It was just so clear that there was no way out of that situation except to get into it. No helicopter was going to come; they were not going to haul me up on the rope; I was not going to float down. I had to get into it, and my feet started to move.

Why would anyone ever want to take the inner journey about which Annie Dillard and Vaclav Havel write? The answer is: There is no way out of my inner life so I'd better get into it. On the inward and downward spiritual journey, the only way out is in and through.

Out of the Shadow, into the Light

The shadow lives of leaders are inevitably projected onto institutions and society. If they are to create less shadow and more light, leaders need to ride certain monsters all the way down. I have five of them as a sampler, and a few thoughts on how the inner journey might transform our leadership at these five points.

One of the biggest shadows inside a lot of leaders is deep insecurity about their own identity, their own worth. That insecurity is hard to see in extroverted people. But the extroversion is often there precisely because they are insecure about who they are and are trying to prove themselves in the external world rather than wrestling with their inner identity.

This insecurity takes a specific form that I have seen many times, especially in men, and I see it in myself: We have an identity that is so hooked up with external, institutional functions that we may literally die when those functions are taken away from us. We live in terror of what will happen to us if our institutional identity were ever to disappear.

When leaders operate with a deep, unexamined insecurity about their own identity, they create institutional settings that deprive *other* people of *their* identity as a way of dealing with the unexamined fears in the leaders themselves.

Here is a simple example. I am astonished at the number of times I call an office and hear "Dr. Jones's office; this is Nancy speaking." The boss has decreed it be done that way. The leader has a title and a last name; the person who answers the phone has neither. This is a small but powerful example of depriving someone else of an identity in order to enhance your own.

Everywhere I look I see institutions depriving large numbers of people of their identity so that a few people can enhance theirs. I look at schools and I see hundreds of thousands of students passively memorizing information delivered by experts. These students have been deprived of an identity by the educational system so that teachers can have more identity for themselves, as if this were a zero-sum game, a win-lose situation. As I go around the country talking to people in higher education, I always ask students, "When was the last time that you were asked to relate your life story to the things you are studying?" They say, "What? Our life story doesn't count here." The whole idea in higher education is to replace their "little" life stories with the "big" story of the disciplines. The whole idea in an expert-dominated, technocratic form of education is to devalue those little parochial stories on behalf of the "true" one. And think of what we do to patients in a hospital. Talk about depriving people of identity so that leaders can have more for themselves!

It is not always this way. There are organizations led by people who know who they are "all the way down," whose identity does not depend on a specific role that might be taken away at any moment. If you are in that kind of organization, you are with people and in settings that *give* you identity, that empower you to be someone. I think that is a core issue in the spirituality of leadership. The great spiritual gift that comes as one takes the inward journey is to know for certain that who I am does not depend on what I do. Identity does not depend on titles, or degrees, or function. It depends only on the simple fact that I am a child of God, valued and treasured for what I am. When a leader knows that, then the classroom is different, the hospital is different, and the office is different.

The second shadow of leadership that is inside a lot of us (and please understand that I am talking about myself and my struggles here as much as anybody else's) is the perception that the universe is essentially hostile to human interests and that life is fundamentally a battleground.

Have you ever noticed how often people use "battle" images as they go about the work of leadership? We talk about "do or die" tactics and strategy, about using our big guns, about allies and enemies, about wins and losses. The imagery suggests that if we fail to be fiercely competitive, we will lose, because the basic structure of the universe is a vast combat. The tragedy of that inner shadow, that unexamined inner fear of failing, is that it helps create situations where people actually have to live that way.

Our commitment to competition is a self-fulfilling prophecy. Yes, the world is competitive, but only because we make it that way. Some of the best operations in our world, some of our best corporations, some of our best schools, are learning that there is another way of going about things, a way that is consensual, cooperative, communal. They are fulfilling a different prophecy and creating a different reality.

The spiritual gift we receive as we take the inward journey is the knowledge that the universe is working together for good. The universe is not out to get anybody; the structure of reality is not the structure of a battle. Yes, there is death, but it is part of the cycle of life, and when people learn to move with that cycle there is coherence and great harmony in our lives. That is the spiritual insight that can transform this particular dimension of leadership and thus transform our institutions.

The third shadow in leaders I call "functional atheism"—the belief that ultimate responsibility for everything rests with *me*. It is the unconscious, unexamined conviction within us that if anything decent is going to happen here, I am the one who needs to make it happen.

Functional atheism leads to dysfunctional behavior on every level of our lives: workaholism, burnout, stressed and strained and broken relationships, unhealthy priorities. It is the reason the average group can tolerate only fifteen seconds of silence; people believe that if they are not making noise, nothing is happening!

The great gift we receive on the inner journey is the certain knowledge that ours is not the only act in town. Not only are there other acts in town, but some of them, from time to time, are even better than ours. On this inner journey we learn that we do not have to carry the whole load, that we can be empowered by sharing the load with others, and that sometimes we are even free to lay our part of the load down. We learn that co-creation leaves us free to do only what we are called and able to do, and to trust the rest to other hands.

The fourth shadow among leaders is fear. There are many kinds of fear, but I am thinking especially of our fear of the natural chaos of life. Many leaders have a deep devotion to eliminating all remnants of chaos from the world. They want to order and organize things so thoroughly that the nasty stuff will never bubble up around us—such nasty stuff as dissent, innovation, challenge, change. In an organization, this particular shadow gets projected outward as rigidity of rules and procedures. It creates corporate cultures that are imprisoning rather than empowering.

What we forget from our spiritual traditions is that chaos is the precondition to creativity. Any organization (or any individual) that does not have a safe arena for creative chaos is already half dead. When a leader is so fearful of chaos as not to be able to protect and nurture that arena for other people, there is deep trouble. The spiritual gift of the inner journey is to know that creation comes out of chaos, and that even what has been created needs to be turned to chaos every now and then so that it can be recreated in a more vital form. The spiritual gift on this inner journey is the knowledge that people and organizations not only survive but thrive in chaos, that there is vitality in the play of chaotic energy.

The final example of the shadows that leaders can project on others involves the denial of death. We live in a culture that simply does not want to talk about things dying. Leaders everywhere demand that they themselves, and the people who work for them, artificially maintain things that are no longer alive, maybe never have been. Projects and programs that should have been laid down ten years ago are still on the life-support system.

There is fear in this denial of death—the fear of negative evaluation, the fear of public failure. Surprisingly, the people in our culture who are least afraid of death, in this sense, are the scientists. The scientific community really honors the failure of a hypothesis because the death of an idea produces new learning. But in many organizations, if you fail at what you are doing, you will find a pink slip in your box. Again, the best organizations and leaders are asking people to take risks that may sometimes lead to failure, because they understand that from failure we can learn.

The spiritual gift on the inner journey is the knowledge that death is natural and that death is not the final word. The spiritual gift is to know that allowing something to die is also allowing new life to emerge.

Can we, should we, help each other deal with the spiritual issues inherent in leadership? We *must* help each other because these are critical issues. The failure of leaders to deal with their own inner lives is creating conditions of real misery for lots and lots of folks and unfulfilled missions for lots and lots of institutions. Too many organizations in our society are in deep trouble around the leadership shadows I have tried to name. One way out of trouble is for us to start helping each other recover the power of the inner journey. How might that happen?

To begin, we could strive to elevate the value of "inner work." It would be wonderful if the phrase "inner work" could become a central term in our schools, in our businesses, and in our churches—if we could help people understand that the phrase really means something. The activities that constitute "inner work" are as real and as important as any outer project or task— activities like journaling, reflective reading, spiritual friendship, and meditation. We must come to understand that if we skimp on our inner work, our outer work will be diminished as well.

A second thing we can do is to remind each other that while inner work is a deeply personal matter, it is not necessarily a *private* matter. There are ways to come together in community to help each other with that inner work. I have been very touched by the Quaker tradition, where they know how to come together in support of people engaged in deep inner work. They come together in a way that is supportive but not invasive, that asks a lot of probing questions but never renders judgment or gives advice. They come together in a way that respects the mystery of the human heart but still allows people to challenge and stretch one another in that mystery.

In a beautiful little book called *Letters to a Young Poet,* the German poet Rainer Maria Rilke has a definition of love that still astounds me.[4]

> Love is this—that two solitudes border, protect, and salute one another.

This is the essence of being together in inner work. It avoids the invasive and violent notion that we have in our culture of "getting in there and fixing each other up." It affirms the possibility of being present to a person's solitude, a person's mystery, while that deep inner work goes on.

I wish I had time to tell you, as a person who has struggled through two bouts of that deep inner work called depression, about the healing that came as a few people found ways to stand at the border of my solitude in that experience. Because they were not driven by their own fears to either "fix" or abandon me, they provided lifelines to the human community. It *is* possible for people to be together that way—if we have education for leadership that is not simply about the skills to manipulate the external world but also the personal and corporate disciplines of the inner world.

Finally, we need to remember that all of the great spiritual traditions at their core say one simple thing: Be not afraid. They do not say you cannot *have* fears; we all have fears, and leaders have fears aplenty. But they say you do not have to *be* your fears; you do not have to lead from fear and thus create a world in which fear dominates the lives of far too many people. We can lead, instead, from an inner place of trust and hope, thus creating a world that is more hopeful and more trustworthy.

Notes

1. An earlier version of this chapter appeared as a pamphlet entitled *Leading from Within: Reflections on Spirituality and Leadership,* published by the Indiana Office for Campus Minorities in Indianapolis with support from the Lilly Endowment, 1990.
2. V. Havel, "The Revolution Has Just Begun," *Time* (Mar. 5, 1990): 14–15.
3. A. Dillard, *Teaching a Stone to Talk* (New York: Harper & Row, 1982), 94–95.
4. R. M. Rilke, *Letters to a Young Poet* (New York: Vintage Books, 1987), 78.

3

A Leader's Conscience

The Integrity and Spirituality of Vaclav Havel

John C. Haughey, S.J.

*T*he theme of this book is both unique and insightful. The more I reflected on it the more I was attracted to the thought of writing about the charismatic figure of Vaclav Havel, the playwright who is now president of the Czech republic. Spirituality, leadership, and organizational life are so well integrated in him that he embodies the book's three themes superbly. But you should be warned at the outset of this chapter that Havel's form of leadership is unique. He was and is a meaning maker more than an action taker. His gifts, at least to date, are more in the area of naming the reality he sees rather than managing its changes. His leadership grew out of a conscience pricked by the absurdity of life in Czech society from the 1950s through the 1980s, and his spirituality matured to the point that his readers and compatriots called for and effected the changes he named. His personal integrity has made him the figure with the greatest moral authority in his country since the fall of communism, which led to his election in 1993 to the presidency of the Czech republic.

To understand Havel's role in Czech society, an overview of the country's more recent history is necessary. Czechoslovakia had been under communist rule since 1948, but in the 1960s a cautious movement began working to liberalize the society. When the country's economy stagnated in the late 1960s, liberal Slovak communists seized the moment to replace hard-line leader Antonin Novotny with Alexander Dubcek as the first secretary of the communist party in January of 1968. Under Dubcek's leadership, freedoms increased. Censorship of the press diminished, and other liberalizing reforms were initiated. These reforms became known as the Prague Spring because many of them were initiated in the spring of 1968. Dubcek's ultimate aim was to establish "socialism with a human face" in Czechoslovakia. Then on August 20, 1968, Soviet tanks entered the country by night to end what Soviet leaders described as a "counterrevolution" by "imperialist forces." Dubcek's experiment with socialist democracy ended that evening.[1]

By April of 1969, he was formally replaced by Gustav Husak, who quickly moved to restore the former brand of Soviet-style communism. The aftermath was a sharp reversal of Dubcek's reforms, along with a purge of party members and liberal artists, educators, writers, and economists. Dissidence all but disappeared until the late 1970s. In a very brief outburst in 1977, Czech dissidents, led by Havel, published a manifesto called the Charta 77 protesting the oppression of human rights in their country. The state's response was swift, with detention for all of the manifesto's signers. Little progress on reforms followed until Gorbachev's rise to power in the 1980s, when the liberalization movement was restored during what came to be known as the Velvet Revolution.[2]

Biographical Overview

The last thing the young Havel wanted to be was a leader. His heroes in his early life were playwrights whose genre was the theater of the absurd. Writers of this kind of drama do not take it upon themselves to change society. They do not even purport to know much about what ought to be changed. What they do claim to know and see and name is the absurdity of the conditions of their lives—waiting, they would say, without hope for an unknown something that will never come.

Havel spent his playwright years content to name what was in the air, but his talent for naming has become trenchant as he has moved beyond the theater of the absurd and into the theater of the meaning of our modern dilemma. He has become an outstanding cultural critic, partly because he approaches his task with the sensitivity of an artist rather than with the heavy categories of an academic. From his position as a political leader, Havel is an outspoken critic of his own society, and increasingly of Western society as well.

Born in 1936, he came to know totalitarianism early, first under the Nazis, then under the Soviet Union. He was in his early thirties when he became very much a part of the ferment that gave rise in 1968 to the series of reforms of the Prague Spring. Like all other Czechoslovaks, he was enraged by the tanks that in August finally crushed these political, religious, and cultural enthusiasms. But unlike most of his colleagues, he was not daunted by or silent about his disgust.

Nineteen seventy-seven was a critical year in his life and in the life of the country. It was the year of the formation of Charta 77, an insubordinate caucus aimed at democratizing Czech society via strong advocacy of human rights. It was also the year he was sentenced to ten years in prison for his leadership in rallying the Charta's supporters, known as "refusniks" for their refusal to accept the policies of the day. In 1983 he was released from prison because of illness. Then in 1989, the Velvet Revolution realized its goals with the Civic Forum, a successor to Charta 77. The forum successfully negotiated the demise of the Soviet hegemony over Czechoslovakia. In 1990 Havel was elected president of the country. In 1992 the country bifurcated, becoming two countries, Slovakia and the Czech republic. In February 1993 Havel assumed the presidency of the Czech republic.

These facts are indicators of Havel's leadership, but where is the evidence of his spirituality? It was not until he was in prison that his spirituality began to be articulated, and for a thoroughly practical reason. If he had insisted on writing in the general genre of cultural critique he had carried on before his imprisonment, his letters would have been destroyed by the prison censors. All he could safely communicate were his interior sentiments. It is in the expression of these to his wife, collected in the book *Letters to Olga,* that we come to understand the spiritual depths of Havel.

Havel became a leader of his people in a circuitous, uncalculated way. His spirituality enabled him to take stock both of himself and of his society in each of its organized arrangements. Before he was asked to lead, he was able to contrast the way things were with what could and should be. What he set out to do—to critique society through his writings and speeches—was one thing; what he ended up doing—leading a nation—because he did what he did well, was the last thing he had in mind.

An Overview of His Ideas

Havel has stated that all of his writings, from his plays through his essays, have been about the crisis of identity from which all modern people suffer. He believes that one of the pervasive influences creating this crisis of identity is fear, the fear of losing something. He has traced this bondage of fear to a consumer society that shaped its citizens into a "consumer herd" and rendered them so small-minded that the only world that mattered was the little world of oneself and one's family. "By nailing a man's whole attention to the floor of his mere consumer interests, it is hoped to render him incapable of appreciating the ever-increasing degree of his spiritual, political and moral degradation."[3]

The effect of this pervasive fear in individual citizens was inertia, apathy, and eventually despair. Even more deleterious, according to Havel, was the pretended conformity, the seeming willingness of workers to go through their routines without any commitment to what they were responsible for. As some cynic over in the Soviet Union is said to have quipped at the time, "We pretend to work; they pretend to pay us."

Havel was convinced there was no way out of this impasse of cultural mediocrity in what was becoming a spiritual wasteland, unless people acted according to their consciences. He looked north and saw the effect on Poland of a Walesa; he looked east and saw the effect on the Soviet Union of a Sakharov; he looked back and remembered the effect on both East and West of a Solzhenitsyn.

The political and social impact of people acting on the basis of their consciences deeply impressed Havel. With their example in mind, plus that of the many dissidents in his own country, he concluded that Czechoslovakia's renewal would not happen from the outside in but only from the inside out. Political restructuring would not come about through political means but only through people of conscience standing up for their convictions. As it turned out, he was right. The Velvet Revolution toppled tyranny.

His favorite imagery for describing the spiritual state of Czechoslovakia was that much of the population preferred to live their uneventful lives in the lie they knew rather than in the truth that they could easily have known from their conscience. The catalyst for splitting the population into opposing camps was a rock band in Prague that called itself the Universe of the Plastic People. Even though the band claimed that all they wanted to do was to play their songs, they ran into trouble with the authorities because the lyrics contained seditious ideas, or so the authorities thought. When the reformers rallied to the side of the musicians, the convergence created Charta 77, which did for Czechoslovakia what Solidarity had done for Poland. It gave the reformers in the population a cause that enabled them to transcend lives of mediocrity and fear.

Still, even though there was a discernible community of refusniks who could count on one another, the regime did not topple immediately. There were two reasons for this. The first was the memory of the crushing of the Prague Spring of 1968 and a fear of its repeat. But even more daunting, Havel believed, was the damnable proclivity of human beings to create systems and then do everything in their power to maintain them long after their authenticity and value disappeared, if indeed there had ever been any value there in the first place. The core perversity here was the refusal of individuals to take responsibility for personal and organizational renewal. Instead, responsibility was avoided; in fact, it was ideologically denied by having it subsumed into maintaining the system. The net effect of a critical mass yielding to this temptation was a deeply demoralized people.

This was economism pure and simple, to import a favorite word of Pope John Paul II, which means a culture trivialized by values that never transcend an economic paradigm. But this was only one level of the explanation of the sorry state of Czech society. The deeper and more universal explanation for the malaise, according to Havel, was that Czechoslovakia, like much of modern society, was "living in the middle of the first atheistic civilization." The effect of this was an "arrogant anthropocentrism" that had lost touch with any transcendent reality.[4] The irony here was that at the moment human beings placed themselves at the summit of meaning in the world and took themselves to be the measure of everything, their economies began to take the measure of them.

By not living in a way that was open to transcendence, Havel saw his country committing a kind of megasuicide. He was sure that humanity needed to live in a hope "anchored somewhere beyond the world's horizons" in order to live responsibly. Given a horizon of transcendent hope, human beings can and should "be the measure of all structures including economic structures and not be made-to-measure for those structures."[5]

There is, then, a mutuality in a given society: its organizations are only as healthy as its culture, and its culture is only as healthy as its organizations. A healthy culture enables its citizens to "enlarge their liberty and discover their truth."[6] Absent such a culture, people begin to accede to the lies told them by those with an interest in maintaining the lie. They live in a culture that is self-deceived and work in organizations that are also self-deceived.

Havel keenly felt his country growing coarser and coarser. "The worst future of the crisis is that it keeps deepening . . . how hastily we are all abandoning positions which only yesterday we refused to desert. What social conscience only yesterday regarded as improper is today casually excused; tomorrow it will eventually be thought natural, and the day after be held up as a model of behavior. . . . As our insensitivity has increased, so naturally our ability to discern our own insensitivity has declined."[7]

Letter to Husak

We can appreciate how far beyond the theater of the absurd Havel had come by reading his 1975 letter to Gustav Husak, then general secretary of the Czechoslovak communist party. Like many of Havel's writings, the letter reveals the broad reach of his cultural criticism.

He warned the general secretary that there was an almost universal despair about setting public affairs right. The deep pessimism that pervaded the country was obscured because on the surface things seemed tolerable. But that was because people had decided there was nothing they could do to bring truth or justice to public life and instead busied themselves with their own careers, families, and the endless purchase of home accoutrements. "It is the worst in us which is being systematically activated and enlarged—egotism, hypocrisy, indifference, cowardice, fear, resignation and the desire to escape every personal responsibility."[8]

While apathy and the fear that was its source suffused the land, the managers, who were no less fear ridden lest they lose what little power they had, sought to maintain a semblance of order. It was this seeming order that Havel loathed for its superficiality, its surface consolidation. It was an order without life, a bureaucratic order "of grey monotony" that was "calm as a morgue."[9]

It is not that there is no unity in our society, Havel observed, but it is the "unity of total pretense." The pretense is made possible by the authorities' distrust of variety, uniqueness, and "the restlessness of transcendence," as he picturesquely calls it.[10] He also notes that if there were freedom and trust of those gifted enough to see through the conformity and name the realities operating in the culture, Czech society would begin to pull itself out of its morass.

The Power of the Powerless

In his essay "The Power of the Powerless," written in 1978, Havel began to reflect on what an ideology is and does, at least the ideology extant in his country. His concern was with the success the Soviet ideology was having on his fellow citizens. They had consigned their consciences and their sense of responsibility to a higher authority, the state. This enabled them to live in "the illusion of an identity, of dignity, of morality" without even knowing that all three had been lost.[11] He did not waste his energy blaming the purveyors of the ideology. His complaint was with those who used it as an excuse, hiding behind it, not admitting the trivialization of their lives under the regime, adapting to the status quo after the manner of cowards.

So, on the one hand the ideology generated a kind of coherence, and on the other hand it had become a source of excuses for the populace. Its excusatory function in effect says, This is the way we do things here; this is the way things are here; this is the way things will stay. Consequently, one goes through the motions while remaining uninvested in the outcomes. Ideology creates a system of rituals. Ideology does not require belief in its premises, only conformity to its operations. One's conformity is a sign of one's decision to "live within the lie." In doing so, one not only confirms the system but fulfills it, makes it. In fact "you are the system," Havel witheringly pointed out.[12] As long as you perform the expected rituals, you are both an object in a system of control and subject as well. You are both a victim of the system and its instrument.

But living within the ideology's lie creates a system only if it is universally acquiesced in, only if it embraces and permeates every individual and organization within its orbit. Consequently, anyone who steps outside the system or outside predetermined roles threatens the system in its entirety, because the refusnik in effect is saying that the truth lies elsewhere.

Havel warns that those whose job is overseeing this

world of appearances will go all out to manhandle, marginalize, expel, or exterminate dissidence so that the specious unity over which they preside may be maintained. The system cannot afford to have some of its subjects take responsibility back into themselves and pursue aims that are generated elsewhere. The threat is expressed in spatial terms by Havel. To live within the truth moves the center of gravity away from the political and its structures to the prepolitical, where life begins to develop its own postideological dynamics.[13]

Once people or organizations turn away from living the lie and from the inexorable entropy that accompanies it, they face into truth and life. Life has its own aim; life has diversity, independent self-constitution, plurality, fulfillment of dreams. It is marked with a high degree of emancipation. Its devotees "sail upon a vast ocean of the manipulated life like little boats, tossed by the waves but always bobbing back as visible messengers of living within the truth, articulating the suppressed aims of life."[14] Intentionally or unintentionally, the dissenters lived their lives in the service of truth because they made room for the genuine aims of life. In his 1975 letter to Husak, Havel had put it more graphically: "Life cannot be destroyed for good; a secret streamlet trickles on beneath the heavy crust of inertia and pseudo-events, slowly and inconspicuously undermining it."[15]

As the dissidents reached critical mass, a parallel culture came into being and began to develop its own organizational forms. For example, the powerful *samiz-*

dat underground developed its own way of publishing and distributing the literature that the authorities found seditious. The new parallel system pursued and embodied new values, such as trust, hope, solidarity, openness, and responsibility. Havel warned that this state of affairs could not go on for long. Parallel systems could not long coexist. In his own life this warning was fulfilled with his imprisonment for his role as a leader of the dissidents.

Politics and Conscience

Havel's belief in politics is evident in his essay written in 1984, "Politics and Conscience," his first major piece after his release from prison. But the politics he believed in was politics from below, politics rising up from consciences pricked by the agendas set by life, politics that grows out of real needs, not the need to maintain existing ideology. This new politics was intensely personal. Its power came from the autonomous, integral, dignified human "I" that was bound to something higher, to its absolute horizon.

Traditional politics, in contrast, had become impersonal. Where did this impersonal power get its force? Havel traced it not to Karl Marx, as we might guess, but all the way back to Machiavelli and his analysis of power. Machiavelli, according to Havel, separated power from the source of power, the human person. Once this was so in conception, it became so in fact. Power began to be used *against* people not *by* people. It was impersonal, even antipersonal. Humanity was transformed into statistics. Impersonal power, the "wellspring of totalitarian thought," generates every kind of repression.[16] Good and evil, which are categories of the natural world, lose their meaning, and quantification becomes the sole measure of the human.

Havel was not an anarchist. He believed in organizations, in structures, in institutions. His problem was with the way these operated in his society, with their distance from the personal power of people they purported to serve. If people were in touch with their own consciences, they would freely invest themselves in creating structures and organizations to meet human needs.

The Spirituality of Vaclav Havel

So far we can hear Havel saying that inauthentic people create inauthentic organizations and societies, and that these in turn generate inauthentic people. He was able to see through this circle that began as a source of mediocrity and ended up demoralizing a whole nation. As Havel matured, he was able to probe his spiritual depths. We have the authorities who imprisoned him to thank for creating—unwittingly, of course—the occasion for him to articulate the deeper probes. The dynamics of human beings as he experienced them are ably conveyed in his letters to his wife, Olga, written between 1979 and 1982. These letters spell out his spirituality.

Havel was a believer in God, though a most nontraditional God, and he used several circumlocutions as his preferred way of naming God. One of these was the image of the horizon. "Ever since childhood I have felt that I would not be myself if I did not live in a permanent and manifold tension with this horizon of mine, the source of meaning and hope. And ever since my youth, I've never been certain whether this is an experience of God or not."[17]

Pondering the unclarity, he goes on to say: "Whatever it is [that I am experiencing], I do not worship this god-of-mine and I don't see why I should . . . [since] it seems quite absurd to me that this intimate-universal partner of mine—who is sometimes my conscience, sometimes my hopes, sometimes my freedom and sometimes the mystery of the world—might demand to be worshipped or might even judge me according to the degree to which I worship him."[18]

After his release, Havel was asked if he had converted to Catholicism while in prison. He answered: "It depends on how we understand conversion." If it means "replacing an uncertain something with a completely unambiguous personal God, and fully, inwardly, to accept Christ as the son of God, along with everything that entails, including the liturgy [then] I have not taken that step." He continued: "There are some things that I have felt since childhood: that there is a great mystery above me which is the focus of all meaning and the highest moral authority; that the event called the 'world' has a deeper order and meaning and therefore is more than just a cluster of improbable accidents; that in my own life I am reaching for something that goes far beyond me and the horizon of the world that I know;

that in everything I do I touch eternity in a strange way."[19]

He was loath to speak of his relationship with God; perhaps he might never have thought about it in a formal way if he had not been forced to focus on it in his long prison hours. Even then he was unhappy with the expressions he found available to him to describe God. They were, to his distress, "abstract and vague" whereas his relationship with God was "vivid, intimate and particular, thanks to its constantly astonishing diversity."[20]

Havel prefers to refer to God as Being. He recoils from a religious faith that is graspable or, as he calls it, "reified," in the sense of completed, something given for all time and no longer mystery. Such a God, Havel protests, would be too small, especially if the requirement of belief was that God had to be served. He resists believing in religion with its tradition of doctrines if that means that one does not need to constantly go back over elementary questions. Such a reification ceases to be a faith and becomes a mere clinging, oriented toward entities, things, and objects. He sees such a faith as a covert way of surrendering, not to God but to the world.

In this connection, he has an unforgettable analysis of the difference between faith and fanaticism. The essence of the fanatic's error is to think that one can transfer "primordial self-transcendence from the boundlessness of the dream to the reality of human actions in a one-shot affair . . . to be relieved of the duty and effort of constantly aspiring toward Being; for in its place there is a handy substitute . . . the relatively undemanding duty of devoted service to a given project." He derides fanaticism as a "reified, mystified, fetishized, and thus, self-alienated faith." It "replaces a difficult orientation toward Being with a more facile orientation toward the human product, claiming exclusive rights to mediate contact with Being." He describes fanaticism as "wrapping its existential nakedness, and its exhausting, lifelong openness to questions, in the flag of its own responses; fanaticism may make life simpler—but at the cost of hopelessly destroying it."[21]

The issue of responsibility looms large in Havel's mature thought. He believes it was the evolving objects of his responsibility that brought him to God gradually over time. Responsibility is the thing that matures a person, he is convinced. There is no real identity unless and until one takes responsibility. For him this took place in stages. His first sense of responsibility was to and for the environment. His next was to his transcendent conscience or inner voice. Finally, he concluded that these were simply different ways in which he was in contact with a higher authority.

Not only do we come to our identity through taking responsibility, but we also come to God the same way. "To whom are we responsible? I don't know 'to whom,' but it is certainly not, in the final instance, to any of the transitory things of this world. It follows that I am convinced that the primary source of all responsibility, or better still, the final reason for it, is the assumption of an absolute horizon. It is precisely responsibility—as the bearer of continuity and thus of identity, that is the clearest existential reflection or pledge in man of the permanence and absoluteness of the absolute horizon of Being."[22]

One particular letter to Olga began with a personal anecdote. Havel wondered why in traveling in a conductorless streetcar in Prague he had bothered to drop his fare in the box when no one would have known whether he did. He was sure he knew why he and everyone else do bad. What intrigued him was why he and the rest of us do good. He concluded that "there is something in man that compels him to behave (to a degree, at least) as though someone were constantly observing him. And if he does something he shouldn't in such a situation, he may even engage in a kind of dialogue with the 'observer,' pleading his own case and attempting, in all manner of ways, to explain and apologize for his own behavior." We carry within ourselves, he is sure, an "inner experience of the total integrity of Being."[23] This intuition links conscience both to God and to integrity. Being is the only reality with integrity; obeying one's conscience brings one into communion with this "integrity of Being."

Havel describes the precise moment when he was able to put these three realities together. On a hot summer day he was sitting on a pile of rusty iron and gazing beyond the prison walls at an enormous tree. As he watched its trembling leaves against the backdrop of endless sunny sky, "I seemed to rise above all the coordinates of my momentary existence in the world into a kind of state outside of time in which all the beautiful things I had ever seen or experienced existed in a total 'co-present.'" At that moment he felt "a profound amazement at the sovereignty of Being" and felt himself "tumbling endlessly into the abyss of its mystery" as well as "an unbounded joy at being alive, at having been given the chance to live through all I have lived through" and see "a deep and obvious meaning" in all these events. He describes the feeling of "standing at the edge of the finite . . . flooded with a sense of ultimate happiness and harmony with the world and myself." Indeed he boldly states that at that moment "I was somehow struck by love, though I don't know precisely for whom or what." Nonetheless, he is sure that what he experienced at that moment was "an echo of the as yet unfamiliar theme from the symphony of Being."[24]

In later letters, he sorts out even further this experience of what he was to call "genuine contact." God, he stresses again and again, is Being, a personal Being who has and is integrity. He sees himself and all of us "longing for Being" and longing for its integrity at the same time. "Evidently there exists an experience in which the longing of separated Being, for reemerging with the integrity of Being is satisfied, as it were, in the most mature and complete manner." This longing shows itself most clearly in an unending search for meaning. "Does not the hunger for meaning, for an answer to the qustion of what—in the process of becoming ourselves—we have become, derive from the recollection of a separated being for its state of primordial being in Being?"[25]

It seems that Havel's most notable contribution to his country has been his ability to satisfy its hunger for meaning. He has done so by tracing the hunger back to its source, God, which he prefers to name in philosophical terms, Being. Havel gets from Heidegger the idea that we are in our individual selves thrown out into existence, away from the Being to which we initially, prenatally, were attached. He is aware in himself of an "endless, boundless and unreserved, prerational and prerationalized responsibility for another and for others" and traced this back to the fact that "separated being remembers its ancient being-in-Being."[26] The greatest challenge of life, Havel is certain, is to reemerge with this Being from whom we are separated. An appetite for this reemergence comes from our existential sense of being alienated from ourselves, the world, and one another in our everyday lives. The three ways available to us to move in the direction of the reemergence back into the integrity of Being are being responsible for more than ourselves, being attuned to what our consciences are saying, and engaging in an endless pursuit of meaning.

European philosopher Emmanuel Levinas's writings had awakened Havel to the centrality of responsibility-to-the-other, both for personal identity and for transcendence, which Levinas called vertical transcendence. In fact, it has been Havel's peculiar kind of vertical transcendence that has enabled him to critique both religiosity and ideology. He has resisted totalism from whatever source. He does not believe in the horizontal revolution of socialism any more than he believes in the horizontal revolution of religious fanaticism. Instead, he believes that taking responsibility for oneself and the other as well as for the whole "leads man to a permanent and permanently deepening relation with the integrity of Being." The introspective prisoner commented that "because [the human being] is rooted in Being by virtue of its origins, it carries that loss within it as part of its own essence" and consequently experiences a "homesickness for the integrity of Being." We experience an "irrepressible need to go beyond all situational horizons, to ask questions, to know, to understand, to get to the bottom of things."[27]

Havel, who is still producing cultural criticism, has become increasingly aware in the last few years that he was speaking about more than his own culture and its organizations—he was describing the social and cultural condition of much of the West. His leadership is all the more remarkable because it was so effective when he had virtually no voice at all. And now that his country has split into two, his voice is gaining a wider, international audience as people begin to understand that he has been naming realities that are true of their own cultures. His is the power of words, words that are true and that take courage to say. They have power because they come from depths that his contemporaries are so often incapable of plumbing in themselves.

Notes

1. M. A. Bacheller (ed.), *The Hammond Almanac* (Maplewood, N.J.: Hammond Almanac, 1983), 559.

2. Bacheller, *Hammond Almanac,* 559.
3. J. Vladislav, ed., *Vaclav Havel, or Living in Truth: Twenty-Two Essays* (London: Faber and Faber, 1986), 12.
4. V. Havel, *Disturbing the Peace: A Conversation with Karel Hvizdala* (New York: A. Knopf, 1990).
5. Havel, *Disturbing the Peace,* 11–13.
6. Vladislav, *Living in Truth,* 16.
7. Vladislav, *Living in Truth,* 15–16.
8. Vladislav, *Living in Truth,* 35.
9. Vladislav, *Living in Truth,* 25.
10. Vladislav, *Living in Truth,* 32.
11. Vladislav, *Living in Truth,* 42.
12. Vladislav, *Living in Truth,* 45.
13. Vladislav, *Living in Truth,* 58–59, 61–65.
14. Vladislav, *Living in Truth,* 85.
15. Havel, *Disturbing the Peace,* xii.
16. Vladislav, *Living in Truth,* 143.
17. Vladislav, *Living in Truth,* 189.
18. Havel, *Letters to Olga,* P. Wilson, trans. (New York: Holt, 1989), 101.
19. Vladislav, *Living in Truth,* 189.
20. Havel, *Letters to Olga,* 102.
21. Havel, *Letters to Olga,* 363–364.
22. Havel, *Letters to Olga,* 233.
23. Havel, *Letters to Olga,* 232.
24. Havel, *Letters to Olga,* 331–333.
25. Havel, *Letters to Olga,* 332, 320.
26. Havel, *Letters to Olga,* 323–324.
27. Havel, *Letters to Olga,* 329.

4

Leadership and Spirituality
A Quest for Reconciliation

Katherine Tyler Scott

Achieving consensus on the meaning of *leadership* remains an elusive accomplishment. Nor do we agree on the meaning of *spirituality.* And unlike leadership, which everyone agrees is necessary, we lack certainty about the value and emphasis spirituality should have in our public lives. So an exploration of these two words individually or in combination could be an exercise in frustration, especially for those who seek absolute answers. But it also can provide us with an opportunity to probe each more deeply and perhaps to witness the emergence of something new and even more mysterious. As I embark on this quest I am reminded of Parker Palmer's words in *To Know As We Are Known:* "We must remember that we not only seek truth but that truth seeks us as well."[1]

The problem with coming to know these two words is that our traditional approach to learning frequently prevents the truth from seeking us. Our tendency is to concretize information into distinct, manageable pieces that we often call "facts"; we externalize knowledge as if there is no relationship to the individual seeking it. The learner then becomes an outside observer, striving to honor the distance required for the elimination of any semblance of subjectivity. As Parker so ably expresses it, "The way we know has powerful implications for the way we live. Every mode of knowing contains its own moral trajectory, its own ethical direction and outcomes."[2] Keeping in mind the limitations of objectivism, I think such an approach can serve as a beginning point rather than the sole framework for our exploration.

Dictionary definitions of these two terms demonstrate some of the challenge and dilemma such an exploration holds. *Spirit* is defined as "That which is traditionally believed to be the vital principle or animating force within living beings; that which constitutes one's unseen intangible being; the real sense or significance of something." The definition of *leadership* is "To show the way by going in advance; conduct, escort, or direct; to cause to follow some course of action or line of thought."[3]

Immediately we can see that the objective definitions lead us in different directions: *spirit* evokes images of an intangible and internal world, while *leadership* focuses on the visible and the external reality. Spirit is a matter of being and becoming, of creation and re-creation, while leadership is doing, acting, performing. The definition of *spirit* invites contemplation, analysis, and insight, while that of *leadership* directs our attention to visible results.

It is my contention that coming to a deeper understanding of spirituality and leadership can be facilitated by an exploration of three things: the division we experience between the private and public realms of our lives; our capacity for self-knowledge; and the organizational structures in which we work and live. Such exploration will help us understand the ways in which these two words and their meanings commingle and manifest in our lives.

My work focuses on leadership education in the not-for-profit sector, a sector with significant history and growing influence. There are an estimated 873,000 philanthropic not-for-profits and 370,000 other not-for-profits in the United States. As Michael O'Neill points out, "by any measure—size, economic impact, political influence, cultural role, effect on personal and social values, effect on public policy, or international presence—private non-profit organizations hold a highly important position in American life." . . . [The nonprofit sector] employs more civilians than the federal and state governments, and ranks eighth among world economies." In addition to this vast paid workforce, "an estimated 98.4 million Americans volunteer an average of four hours a week of their time to this sector at an estimated annual cost of $110 billion."[4]

The capacity to address a range of human needs through the organized efforts of thousands of volunteers is one of the unique and impressive American legacies. Much of public policy, the formation of community values, and the development of leadership are shaped in this arena where people from various backgrounds come together to attempt to serve the common good. Attention to the quality of leadership in this sector is critical. It is one of the few places where community can still be experienced in all of its diversity, in all of its messiness. It is a place where the public and private intersect, and where the struggle to merge leadership and spirituality is more easily seen.

The Great Divide:
The Schism Between Private and Public

I believe that the differences between our perceptions of leadership and spirituality, and the struggle we have in connecting them, reflect a serious division in our culture. Pairing these two concepts brings us face to face with a deep schism in our culture that has increased individual alienation and institutional fragmentation. We have made rigid demarcations between our private and our public lives, reserving the spiritual for the private realm and leadership for our professional and public lives. This separation has created psychological and emotional blinders that rob those in management and leadership positions of a view of the whole. It is what enables those with the institutional power to make changes in an organization to use the rational as the primary or sole basis for decision making, a practice that ultimately stifles spirit.

A relevant example is a highly respected institution that found itself in a severe personnel crisis, even though it excelled in every category the business world uses to characterize and measure success—financial solvency, capital expansion and growth, cutting-edge technology, and excellent staff. The director and the trustees of the organization were shocked to learn from an outside evaluation team that staff morale was so low that it headed the list of issues needing immediate attention in the consulting team's report. Efforts to clear up what was immediately labeled a communications problem revealed that well-intended policies developed to improve the organization had been created with minimal input from, or interpretation to, the staff.

The present director had been hired expressly to overcome the deficiencies of his predecessor and had been given a mandate to institute rapid changes to restore the institution to excellence. He accomplished his mandate in a competent and efficient manner. But no attention had been given to helping the staff grieve the loss of colleagues or the differences in work responsibilities and patterns. No room was given for the ambiguity and uncertainty generated by these new changes, so these feelings went underground and festered. People began to disconnect and in that disconnection began to lose a source of energy that could sustain them in difficult times.

It is in and through the connections with others that we gain a fuller sense of who we are and what truth is. The organization's structure and leadership had allowed individuals to separate from their larger context, and losing sight of this relationship led to what I would call a "crisis of spirit." Parker Palmer characterizes the result of this disconnectedness: "There is an illness in our culture: it arises from our rigid separation of the visible world from the powers that undergird and animate it. With that separation we diminish life, capping off its sources of healing, hope, and wholeness."[5]

The intersection of the private and public realms of our lives is the place where spirit and leadership can merge and emerge, where the dichotomy between them can be transformed into paradox, where integration and wholeness can occur. It is the space where people can discover and negotiate the relationship between their private needs, hopes, and aspirations and the needs, hopes, and aspirations of other realities, whether these are in the form of a group, an organization, or an entire community.

Our difficulty in dealing with the division between our private and public lives has contributed to massive anxiety and flight to the familiar, where the obsession with *doing* can camouflage the fears and inadequacies stirred up in the struggle to be whole. The effort to avoid anxiety propels us toward hard-and-fast rules and gives us an illusion of certainty and predictability. It does not move us toward an environment that fosters the development of the courage and skills necessary to encounter and balance the internal and external life. Quelling anxiety and learning to face the new include grappling with different levels of reality, experiencing the tensions of ambiguity and paradox, and balancing private and public life. It involves an awareness of being part of a whole, a whole with visible and invisible parts. It is a recognition of one's existence in the context of Other, and of a sense of interconnectedness to a much larger world.

Self-Knowledge: Embracing Wholeness

Leadership that acknowledges and integrates the spiritual does not flee from the deep divide between the private and public. The capacity to move into the void is directly related to leaders' capacity to deal with their own internal polarities. It is in the integration of the inner and outer worlds that true spirituality can be distinguished from false. But this integration is greatly influenced by an internal struggle in the psyche for balance. From this struggle self-knowledge is attained. The process is comparable to a desert experience—it is a place of encounter, deafening in its silence, terrifying in its solitude, frightening and joyous in its discoveries.

In a culture where the prevailing view of leadership is doing, acting, and performing, it is not surprising to discover that the majority of leadership studies, and our translation of them, focus primarily on the external, on visible results and concrete outcomes. It is easy to find books, articles, and audiovisual tapes that provide instruction on what a leader *does* or enables others *to do*—everything from enhancing physical appearances to empowering others. We have few opportunities to learn how a leader comes to be a person—a whole person. In the plethora of leadership resources, very few invite or help leaders to pursue the inner journey required for self-knowledge.

Whether we believe that leadership is a complex configuration of individual traits, a series of actions or activities, a process of transactions, or some combination of these, the selfhood of the leader is a critical variable in what happens. The overemphasis on the external in our culture has contributed to a devaluing of the internal life of the leader. Self-reflection, exploration, or analysis in any depth is frequently and derisively referred to as "touchy-feely," a characterization that colludes in the continuation of the separation between public and private, and in my view dismisses a discipline that powerfully forms and informs the nature of leadership. This process of reflection and analysis needs to be reclaimed from being the sole preserve of scholars, theologians, philosophers, and therapists.

Jung's concepts of persona, ego, and shadow are helpful in coming to an understanding between self-knowledge and spiritually integrated leadership. Persona is what we envision ourselves to be and how we wish to be seen by the world; it is the mediator between the self and the environment. The ego is what we are and know about consciously. The shadow is that part of us that we fail to see or know. As Jungian analyst Robert A. Johnson notes, "the shadow houses both the refused and unacceptable parts of us and the 'gold' in our personality."[6] The psyche constantly seeks balance and synthesis between the ego and the shadow. The shadow has an energy potential nearly as great as that of the ego, and denying it increases its destructive power.

Our culture has emphasized the development of the ego and persona in leaders—the positive, desirable, and conscious qualities. Denial of the negative aspects in the shadow leads to projection of these qualities onto other individuals, groups, or organizations; and it does not permit the leader an opportunity to work on integrating them into the psyche.

As Robert A. Johnson explains, "it is useful to think of the personality as a teeter totter or seesaw. Our acculturation consists of sorting out our God-given characteristics and putting the acceptable ones in the right side of the seesaw and the ones that do not conform on the left. It is an inexorable law that no characteristic can be discarded; it can only be moved to a different point on the seesaw. A cultured person is one who has the desired characteristic visible on the right (the righteous side) and the forbidden ones hidden on the left. All our characteristics must appear somewhere in this inventory. Nothing may be left out."[7] An inability to struggle honestly with the whole self unwittingly cre-

71

ates circumstances or an environment that is damaging to both the leader and others involved.

Denial of the gold in the shadow can be just as damaging, for it diminishes the leaders' capacity to claim their gifts, higher calling, or constructive creativity. It leads to hero worshipping in which another individual is forced to carry the burden of these gifts.

Leaders out of touch with themselves can contribute to illness and dysfunction of their system. In medical settings the term used is *iatrogenic*, a condition in which the intervention creates the illness. We must be reminded by our spiritual heritage that a powerful partnership exists between our internal world and external reality. In this partnership, both realms are in continuous interaction; each one influences and shapes the other. We are not just being acted upon. We are helping to create the circumstances of our lives.

Leaders who can claim their shadow and face their internal polarities have a better chance of achieving balance and wholeness both inside and outside. They create spaces within and without where spirituality can emerge. When they permit opposites to overlap, they create what is termed a *mandorla,* a symbol of healing and of reconciliation of opposites. Robert A. Johnson observes: "The mandorla binds together that which was torn apart and made unholy. . . . Wholeness comes from the overlap of good and evil, light and dark. It is not that the light element alone does the healing; the place where light and dark begin to touch is where miracles arise."[8]

Structure: Creating Space
for Leadership and Spirit

The way an organization is structured can greatly affect the creation of spaces where wholeness can be nurtured. Two types of organization have a particularly strong influence, one negative and the other positive: the familiar hierarchy, where leadership is automatically linked with those at the top of the pyramid, and the circular structure, where leaders operate from the center of a team. The characteristics of the two types are summarized in Table 4.1, and described in detail in the sections below.

Hierarchy

The prevailing organizational structure—hierarchy—reflects the schism between the private and the public, between self and others, and between leadership and spirituality. In the hierarchy we automatically accord leadership to those in high-status positions. Being in a leadership role and being a leader should not be perceived as synonymous. Leadership solely by virtue of title is frightening because so much is assumed and unchallenged about the person in the position. In this structure leadership is defined by status and connections, rather than by character, self-knowledge, or connectedness to others.

Hierarchy is managed through a set of rules which seek to control rather than empower. The international consultant on organizational behavior Peter Block re-

**Table 4.1. Organizational Structure:
Hierarchy versus the Circle.**

Structure	Hierarchy	Circular
Focus	Position Power Profit Production	People Purpose Renewal Growth
Outcome	Change Action Mastery Conformity	Transformation Being Learning Diversity
Leadership Style	Dominant Management Controlling	Partnership Collaboration Inspiring

minds us: "The reality of our lives and our work is that we are dealing with patriarchal systems in which the rules are control and submission to authority, denial of self-expression, sacrifice, and instrumentality."[9] In this structure the skills that seek to control (management) are of highest importance. In the hierarchy leadership is vested in one person at the top with multiple levels of people and descending levels of power.

The hierarchical structure tends to promote a pernicious individualism that tears at what few threads of community might exist. The tragedy is that the "leader" in this system becomes more isolated from others and is cut off from the information needed to be effective. He or she lacks information from the organizational depths and is much more likely to become out of touch with the connections and relationships between people and issues—the manifestations of the spirit of an organization. In the hierarchy, the leader is often sealed off from the potential of honest, corrective feedback, and those who chronically complain about the leadership as a reason for their own lack of responsibility are in collusion to maintain the very behavior about which they complain.

The prevalent and operative words in the hierarchy are *dominance* and *power.* However, in such a system power is perceived as finite; only a few people have access to it, and fewer still possess it. The expectation for those who wish to succeed in this structure is to acquire power and control. When there is a perception that power is a scarcity, individuals in the system compete in a win-lose arena; someone will win and someone will lose. The language in the system conveys the belief in scarcity and bespeaks the great divide: *over/ under, top/bottom, up/down, superiors/subordinates.* When power is perceived as limited, getting extraordinary things done is nearly impossible.

I worked in a large Midwestern psychiatric hospital right after I finished graduate school. It was a nationally recognized treatment center and training facility for residents in psychiatry, psychology, social work, and nursing students. If there was any doubt about the existence of a hierarchy (or its colleague, bureaucracy), it was soon erased by the physical arrangement of offices, scheduling of rounds, and clinical conferences.

Harrison Owen, an Episcopalian priest and an expert on myth and rituals, believes that our obsession with structure causes us to build structure first and then try squeezing the spirit in. As he says, "Creating structure before attending to spirit is like buying a pair of shoes without measuring your feet."[10] That seemed to be the case in this instance. The arrangement and use of space had little to do with the work of the staff. The social work offices were placed in the basement in rooms with no windows; the psychiatrists were on the top floors. Those below literally could not see out; those above could forget what was below. Although the institution characterized its treatment methodology as a team approach, decision making was solely in the hands of the psychiatrist, and it was he who decided whether others had anything of worth to contribute. The social workers learned that any influence they had came from the psychiatrist, regardless of their experience or competence. In fact on many of these teams the social worker knew more about the patients' psychopathology and the family's social situation. Many felt keenly the lack of congruity between the respectful and caring way they treated patients and the lack of respect they themselves were accorded daily.

The lack of empowerment was indeed dispiriting, and made the ultimate goal of healing a challenging endeavor. Scott Peck describes the potential for the anesthetization of an organization in these circumstances: "Insensitive to our own suffering, we tend to become insensitive to the suffering of others. Treated with indignity, we lose not only the sense of our own dignity, but also the dignity of others."[11] If a primary method for healing damaged psyches is through a therapeutic relationship with the therapist, it is important for the healer to be in an environment that is conducive to healing. This is not to say that excellent care was not provided; in many instances it was, but it was done at a high cost to the caregiver and ultimately to the institution. The energy that normally would go into innovation and creative risk taking was tied up in self-protection.

People who feel powerless, whether they are managers or those being managed, tend to hoard whatever shreds of power they have. Powerless managers tend to adopt petty and dictatorial management styles. They create organizational systems where political skills are essential and passing the buck is the favorite way of handling problems.

The hierarchical structure reinforces the tendency to minimize group accomplishment. The gifts and talents of others are used to make those higher up in the hierarchy look good, rather than recognized as resources to be shared in the service of a larger vision. The spirit of the organization becomes bound up in products to the detriment of process. The bottom line—concrete, measurable results—becomes more important than process, relationships, or building community in relationship with the external world.

Vision in such a system comes from the top and quickly gets translated downward as specific, measurable goals. Those who are responsible for carrying out the vision are seen as technicians rather than co-creators. Instead of building people's capacity to enliven the dream, the structure transforms them into passive drones. In such a system, where success or survival depends on sticking with the predictable rather than risking the possible, spirit and all its attendant energy are repressed. It becomes part of the corporate shadow—a piece of the invisible that cannot be acknowledged and that will ultimately become distorted and expressed in destructive and negative ways.[12]

This is a grim picture, but it exists in far too many organizations. I do not propose eradicating the hierarchy. Even if I did, it would be impossible to do. Its persistence in spite of limitations and increasing criticism means that it provides something the culture values—organization, structure, clarity of roles, predictability, and accountability.

Some questions for those who work in such structures are: How will I choose to use the power I do have? Can I operate within this system without being seduced into behaviors that empower some at the expense of others? How can I nurture my spirit and the spirit of others in an environment that does not honor or value its existence? What is the price I pay to stay in such a system? How long am I willing to pay it?

There is another structure, another way of operating, that holds considerable promise for the connection of leadership and spirit in the workplace: the circular model.

The Circle

The hierarchy is being reformed (stretched, in some instances) into a circle, and this transformation is changing the arena in which leadership operates and develops. In the circular organizational structure, the leader does not operate "on top" of others, but is seen as the enabling center of a team. Formal and informal relationships between people are recognized and appreciated, and differences are valued and respected. There is continuous striving for balance between achievement of organizational goals and the care and development of those who serve the organization. The leader is not expected to be the sole originator of the organization's vision but to listen to emerging ideas and from them to discern and articulate the vision. The leader is expected to be knowledgeable and competent; others are viewed as having skills and important abilities also. Successes in the system are communal, and failure is viewed as an opportunity for learning.

As in the hierarchy, knowledge is power, but in this structure it is power *with,* not power *over.* When this belief prevails in an organization's culture, power is no longer a finite commodity but a resource that can be infinitely created through the act of sharing within community. An abundance of power is perceived, and it becomes the reality. The competency of others is not a threat but a gift beneficial to all. Such a system encourages collaboration and a win/win resolution to differences and conflicts.

I experienced such a structure while employed as a clinical social worker in a private comprehensive psychiatric facility in the East. The organization described itself as a "therapeutic community," and the community included everyone. The usual distinctions in medical or clinical settings were not made between clients and staff. If you walked onto a floor you would not be able to immediately discern by attire who were the recipients of service and who were the service providers. Offices were arranged so that teams were clustered together. Team members were more accessible to one another and communication about patient care was greatly enriched because it was not limited to certain scheduled times.

Decision making was shared, although everyone knew that the psychiatrist was ultimately the person who would be legally liable. Staff members possessed a high energy level that was contagious. Few people watched the clock; they did what was needed to be done in whatever time was needed. People cared about the quality of their own work and that of the larger institution. The focus in this system was on purpose and people, and the product was excellent—clients' needs were met and the quality of staff and services remained high. In the circular structure purpose is best achieved when there is a connectedness between individual purpose and corporate purpose.

The circular structure is predicated on the belief that leadership is transactional, that it depends on the relationship between leaders and followers. It is a relationship based on genuine respect for and valuing of all people and their unique gifts, on a strong sense of mutuality and community, on trust.

Trust is foundational to the health and survival of any organization, and creating and maintaining this trust is the responsibility of the leader. The circular structure is greatly dependent on leadership that can engender trust. The acknowledgment of diversity in this system means that there must be a high level of comfort with managing dissent. Conflict is perceived as an occurrence for strengthening community. The basis of the leaders' capacity to deal with disagreements is that they have a healthy respect for differences and differentness. They genuinely value people of all races and backgrounds. They have a profound awareness of their own prejudices, biases, projections, and insecurities and consciously inventory them in their deliberations, interactions, and decisions.

Some of the primary questions for leaders in this structure are: How can I use and share power in ways that empower and recreate others? How can I ensure creativity and maintain accountability? How can I sustain a culture that values the gifts of all, yet recognizes that all are not equally endowed? How can I have authority independent of title or position? In my valuing of spirit, how can I ensure that the denial of the reality of the shadow side of leadership and organizational life does not occur?

The Missing Piece

In our work with the National Association for Community Leadership and other leadership educational programs, I frequently hear conversations about "something missing" in professional training experiences. Most often this is said in hushed and embarrassed tones, as if people think they should not be feeling this way, given the incredible resources they have been given access to. Most likely these leaders have experienced a fast-paced, intensive, content-laden process. The agendas of these programs appear to be comprehensive—education, economics, employment, government, social services, health care, a sprinkling of skills training, and the increasingly popular topic of the crumbling infrastructure. The predominant format is a parade of major community leaders or experts across the purview of participants, hour after hour, in day-long marathons of objectivism. This ritual is capped off with a minimal debriefing and a social hour. Then all participants return to their positions, where they will soon be absorbed back into familiar hierarchies where bureaucracy reigns.

Because they have been identified as potential leaders they are likely to be tracked. Usually this means their introduction to leadership has been through the narrow and fragmented lens of management. They are placed in a particular position because the organization needs the specific skills they possess. Few of us would argue against matching individual skills with organizational needs. Organizational effectiveness and efficiency increase when this practice is followed, but in this process something very important is frequently left out: matching the organization's reason for being with the individual's sense of purpose. It is this match that deepens commitment and increases the potential of individuals to hold the organization in trust. When we ignore this, we fall into the schism where the private and the public are disconnected. The result of bringing parts of people together with pieces of an organization is a culture where leadership, vision, and commitment are virtually impossible. Something is missing.

Most leaders feel ill prepared for the responsibilities that are expected of them. Many lack a clear sense of their motivations for serving and leading. They know they are expected to be leaders in their organizations and also to serve in the larger community, but there is a limited understanding of why this is important. Outside of their organizations many are trapped in a volunteer hierarchy where they must compete to obtain a seat on one of the more prestigious boards. Something is missing.

In such an environment individual agendas compete with and sometimes supersede organizational mission. There is a great deal of activity but little substantive progress. Noble-sounding goals are set, but without any clear sense of direction or purpose. Decisions are frequently made in a vacuum, with limited insight and virtually no foresight. Parker Palmer writes of the consequences we face: "The private has grown out of proportion in our society, and the inward journey has perverted into narcissism, partly because we have failed to identify their public counterweight."[13]

When I pursue the hushed-tone comments that "something is missing," it does not take long for me to hear that what people are missing in this cacophony of activities is *meaning.* They are seeking connections and connectedness between what they do and who they are. We now have a generation of new and emerging leaders who are experiencing difficulty seeing what is significant and meaningful. The way we helped shape their leadership has not provided them with the tools for bridging the gap of the great divide; in fact the divisions may have widened. Their preparation for leadership has lacked opportunities for in-depth reflection on their own lives and their relationship to the external. They feel divorced from a larger purpose, alienated among a community of doers.

These destructive consequences challenge us to think of different ways of preparing leaders who can help us to bridge these divisions. What is missing? I believe it is the nurturance of spirit.

I have yet to see "nurturance of the spirit" on anyone's staff development agenda, leadership development program, or long-range plan. Even in organizations that use words of the spirit—*vision, mission, team, collaboration, shared leadership*—the emphasis remains primarily on equipping people to *do* rather than helping individuals to understand and connect their own personal mission with that of the organization so that the doing takes on the combined spirit and energy of the integration of private and public. The alignment of the personal with the corporate inspirits individuals and the culture they work in.

How can we help leaders to respond sensitively and comprehensively to the tensions between self-interest and organizational and community needs and interests? If the quality of our private lives affects the quality of organizational and community life, what do we need to do to seed these realms so that they nurture leaders who can create structures and cultures that bring people together in rich, dynamic ways?

Trustee Education: A Process for Integrating Leadership and Spirit

The program I direct works with individuals and not-for-profit organizations to build their capacity to serve and to lead.[14] We have worked with over 2,000 trustees and staff members of not-for-profit organizations using a "depth approach" to the preparation of leadership that we call trustee education. It is an educational process that helps individuals and organizations acquire the lost skills of reflection, analysis, and interpretation of complexity. It enables trustees and staff to explore the deeper levels of their organization's culture and to use this understanding in carrying out their responsibilities of trusteeship and leadership. The process evokes a depth of spirit not only within the organizations but also in the professional consultants who use this process. Our experience causes us to think that processes like ours have the most potential for helping to develop leadership that integrates the spiritual.

Dr. Robert Lynn, former vice president of religion for the Lilly Endowment and the originator of depth education, describes the importance of this approach: "What happens at the deeper levels, the 'subsoil' of institutional life, is finally more significant than any skill training for a particular position. The strength and vitality of an institution arises from the unseen depths.

The best educational programs will help leaders explore the institution's subsoil."[15]

We know that for boards to exercise trusteeship they must be grounded in a knowledge of the larger tradition of their work. They need to learn to discern the broader context within which they make decisions affecting the organization and the larger community. Their decision making can then be further grounded in the context of the organization's history and purpose, its beliefs and values, and an understanding of the larger community in order to position the organization to achieve its vision of the preferred future. Depth education helps trustees blend prudence with creativity, ensuring growth while maintaining organizational integrity. This kind of trustee education equips boards with a process and resources to aid them in recovering trusteeship as a vocation.

Beginning the Process

The process begins with an orientation of board members and staff, an organizational assessment, and historical research and resource development in preparation for a series of intensive experiential sessions (see Figure 4.1). These beginning sessions may be concentrated in a day-and-a-half retreat or spread over several months. Board members research, examine, reflect, discuss, and analyze their organization's history, mission, and publics as preparation for envisioning and planning for the future. Throughout this preliminary process board members are being helped to develop their capacity as "his-

Figure 4.1. Trustee Education Process Cycle.

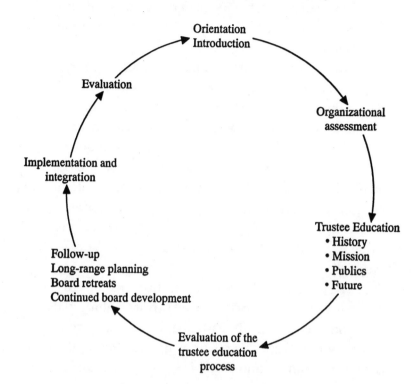

torians, contemporary analysts, and prophets," according to Robert Greenleaf, central and simultaneous roles in carrying out the responsibilities of trusteeship.[16]

During the orientation phase, board and staff are provided an opportunity to explore the question "What does it mean to hold in trust?" Using their understanding of this question they identify someone who has held them in trust. Participants recall personal and professional instances of being held in trust and discuss the

87

qualities and characteristics of the trust holder. The stories are varied and rich. One man remembered that on his first job out of college one of the middle managers took him under his wing and made a major difference in his ability to succeed. A woman recalled loving parents who truly believed in her and "thought she could do anything she set her mind to." Another participant recounted an experience with a third-grade teacher who saw potential in her long before she saw it in herself. These shared experiences of trust holding leave group members feeling a strong sense of caring and of inheriting a legacy of service to others. They grasp the meaning of "holding in trust" at a very personal level before translating its meaning to their capacity to care at an organizational level.

The process addresses the question of connectedness between what happens in the private realm and its effect on one's public life. Participants see in a powerful way how important this relationship has been in their own development and in their sense of service and leadership. Many who experience this process come to a deeper understanding of the commitment, caring, and responsibilities of trust holding because they can begin to see the connection between their own formation and the work they are doing. And they come to a new appreciation of *relationship*—just as they were in relationship with an individual, they are in relationship with an organization. They see that to be a trustee is to be *in relationship,* connected to something larger than any one person, something that includes connections and intersections between people, ideas, and events over time.

History: The Creation
of Organizational Meaning

The capacity to hold an organization in trust is fundamental to trusteeship, and it begins with being knowledgeable about the organization's history. The "lived history" of an organization is the story of its life over time, its trajectory through time. It is a combination of individual and communal stories and of the documented, remembered, and observed history of the organization. It is more than a chronicle of significant people, events, and issues; it is an exploration and interpretation of their relationships to, and their impact on, the organization's character and culture. In a very deep sense, the opportunity to interpret history helps trustees to better comprehend their organization's identity and to create meaning from this information—important abilities of trusteeship. Effective trustee education helps trustees to understand the organization in all its complexity.

During the history session, board members are asked to reflect on up to three different times when their individual lives intersected with that of the organization's: when they first became aware of the organization, when they first became involved, and when they first became a trustee. The discussion leader facilitates the group's analysis of what was going on internally and externally to the organization during these times.

A large historical timeline of the organization is posted on a wall and serves as a visual invitation and reminder to board members to take a broader view, to see things whole. Significant events and people internal

to the organization are written on the bottom of the timeline, significant external events and people on the top.
All participants are asked to sign in twice on the timeline—recording the dates when they first became aware
of the organization and when they became a trustee
of it. Guided by the facilitator, and working in chron-
ological order, each person then recounts the events
of those two times, taking care to note the important
internal and external activities and people. This process moves participants through time and lifts up organizational issues, patterns, strengths, and challenges
more clearly.

The individual stories of board and staff combine
to form the larger organizational story. Trustees learn
to absorb content and interpret context, and in the
process the timeline becomes a symbol of organizational
identity, a powerful representation of culture, a portrait
of the organization within the context of community.
These stories tell us something about the spirit of an
organization. An arts organization board learned that
its indomitable spirit had early origins in the vision and
determination of its founders. They rediscovered this
spirit as they heard the story of setting up the organization's first office in a room the size of a broom closet!

*Mission: The Creation
of Organizational Identity*

The learnings from the first phase of historical analysis
and reflection serve as the foundation for future understanding and decision making. The process next invites

trustees to continue their exploration of the organization's identity and meaning, this time through the lens of mission.

Whom do we serve? For what purpose? These two questions frame the discussion of mission. The process asks trustees to identify the core beliefs and values of the organization, how these are lived out, and their impact. They are asked to look for congruence between what the organization believes and values, whom it serves, and what it does. Board members may also be asked to examine their own beliefs and values, and determine how these intersect with those of the organization. This discussion becomes the foundation for determining their personal stake in the organization.

Board members are introduced to the concept of mission as an overarching purpose and as the standard and measure of organizational congruence and integrity, rather than just a written statement buried in the bylaws or a set of words featured on fundraising literature. The exploration of mission is an opportunity to create organizational identity. Who are we? What are we called to do? The essence and import of mission are eloquently captured by Robert Lynn: "At the root of the creative institution is a shared sense of vocation or, if you prefer, a common calling. In both the Jewish and Christian traditions, the presence of calling is embraced as a gift. The consequences of that gift are evident in a corporate sense of identity and in a unifying loyalty to a set of purposes. If that root sense of mission either has died or is decaying, the whole institution will sooner or later be affected in every respect. Nothing can be more subtle or serious an ailment than this sort of root disease. But whenever an institution undergoes renewal, its new life often springs from a deepened commitment to its vocation."[17]

Mission is the heart and soul of the organization, and a conversation about it becomes an opportunity for board members to be both architects and guardians of the mission. It is the manifestation of organizational spirit, the expression of what it deems to be important.

Publics: The Creation
of Organizational Context

While the session on mission focuses attention on those who are directly served, trusteeship exacts the need for a broader definition and view of publics. Our process engages board members in a historical analysis of publics. A review of the founding and formative events in the organization's life is a reminder that the organization was conceived in response to the needs of a particular group, the public it came into existence to serve.

During the discussion of publics, board members are invited to look at the rich interplay between the organization, issues, events, and people (both internal and external), and to view the organization as a vast web of relationships. This part of the process enlarges the trustees' view of the organization and its interdependence on others. It enables them to see how the organization has related to the community over time.

A "depth" examination of the organization and of

the community in which it lives can serve to minimize organizational tendencies toward isolationism and insularity, and can make it amenable to possibilities of collaboration and partnership. One organization engaged in a trustee education activity that calls for board members to interview people out in the community about the knowledge, understanding, and perceptions of the organization and its programs. All members interviewed a community leader, a parishioner, and a person at large. Because they were willing to hold up a mirror, they received valuable feedback about the need for possible future programs.

Implicit in trust holding is a concern for the common good. We are accustomed to thinking about trustees as being responsible for the health and well-being of the organization they lead, but they have a responsibility to the larger community as well, and the organization is accountable to the larger community through them. To any shared undertaking, trustees bring varying beliefs, values, and opinions about what is best for a community. They act as a permeable membrane—transmitting the needs of the community to the organization, and interpreting the knowledge, identity, and activities of the organization to the community. In this way their decision making occurs within the context of the whole of the community. Trustees link organization and community, ensuring accountability, responsiveness, and credibility.

The discussion of publics is an opportunity for the trustees of an organization to see the bigger picture within which they will be able to make wiser decisions about boundaries of service. It is a reminder of relationship and connectedness to others.

Future: The Creation and Translation of Vision

All organizations depend on the existence of shared meanings and interpretations of reality, and these can be powerfully expressed through an organization's vision. The leader is able to capture the essence of a culture in words, symbols, and metaphor, and to interpret the organization's shared reality and meaning in ways that inspirit the whole. Vision expresses the emotional and spiritual resources of the organization and embodies its values, commitment, and aspirations. Vision calls for the integration of the emotional and spiritual resources of an individual or an organization. It is a choice about how an organization wants its values and beliefs to be lived out, whom it will serve, and what impact it wants to make.

Trusteeship of an organization requires not only a depth of understanding of an organization's past but an ability to envision its preferred future. The session on vision focuses on two processes: visioning and planning. The first prepares trustees to envision what the organization will look like in ten to fifteen years. Then the planning session helps them translate their vision into action. The distinctiveness of the planning process is that it builds on earlier sessions that promoted a deep understanding of history, mission, and publics. Thus the vision is based on, yet transcends, factual reality. The vision is not fantasy, a picture plucked from midair or a figment of imagination. It is rooted in the character, culture, and capacity of the organization.

At this point trustees are prepared for strategic planning. They are equipped with a knowledge and understanding that are foundational to sound planning and decision making. The ability to see beyond the present and to position the organization for both planned and unexpected change is the mark of bold leadership and an important quality of trusteeship.

Continuing the Search

Efforts to acquire and retain an openness to the new and unknown, to seek self-understanding, to embrace the complexity and discomfort of seeing things whole, and to structure one's life and work in ways that connect the internal and the external, the private and the public, the self with other—these are all spiritual acts. In each instance one must be open to the invisible at work and to knowledge that spirituality manifests itself in silence, in an overlapping of opposites through relationships and connectedness. Leaders who practice this have much to teach us.

I am reminded of the story of the five blind men who were given the task of describing an elephant by touching just one part. One man, feeling the trunk, said, "It's a snake!" Another, touching the ear, proudly announced that it was a leaf. Another man thought the elephant's leg was the trunk of a tree. The fourth man

95

was convinced that the side of the elephant was a wall, and the last man, holding the tail, was confident he had a rope. This story is a metaphor for the way in which we have typically viewed spirituality and leadership; our knowledge of them is limited by our individual perspectives. The structured process we call trustee education encourages organizations toward continual learning, a connectedness between the private and public, and a pursuit of the fuller truth. It brings many different perspectives together in an effort to discern deeper meaning and understanding.

This process of disciplined reflection and analysis can also be used with individuals who want to improve their capacity to lead. It helps them identify the origins of their capacity to care for something or someone beyond their own self-interest and provides a way to nurture this spirit in the future. And while it reminds them of the mystery in much of what they do, it also calls them to probe the depths and to persist in the seeking.

We must provide spaces, places, and support for the difficult work of bringing leadership into relationship with spirituality. We must continue to seek and foster processes that bring us new ways of knowing, that allow us to move into the darkness in order to see the light, that take into account the visible and invisible, the subjective and objective, the private and public, as we seek to create ourselves, organizations, and communities.

We would be served well on this journey if we take with us these words from Parker Palmer: "Here is the insight most central to spiritual experience: we are known in detail and depth by the love that created and sustains us, known as members of a community of creation that depends on us and on which we depend. This love knows our limits as well as our potential, our capacity for evil as well as good, the persistent self-centeredness with which we exploit the community for our own ends. Yet, as love it does not seek to confine or manipulate us. Instead it offers us the constant grace of self-knowledge and acceptance that can liberate us to live a larger love."[18]

Notes

1. P. J. Palmer, *To Know As We Are Known: A Spirituality of Education* (San Francisco: Harper & Row, 1983), 72.
2. P. J. Palmer, "Community, Conflict, and Ways of Knowing," *Change* (Sept./Oct. 1987): 22–25.
3. *Webster's Ninth New Collegiate Dictionary* (Springfield, MA: Merriam-Webster, 1987).
4. M. O'Neill, *The Third America: The Emergence of the Nonprofit Sector in the United States* (San Francisco: Jossey-Bass, 1989), 169; B. A. Weisbord, *The Non Profit Economy* (Cambridge, Mass.: Harvard University Press, 1988), 133.
5. Palmer, *To Know As We Are Known*, 10.
6. R. Johnson, *Owning Your Own Shadow* (San Francisco: HarperCollins, 1991). See also C. Zweig and J. Abrams, eds., *Meeting the Shadow* (New York: St. Martins, 1991).
7. Johnson, *Owning Your Own Shadow*, 11.

8. Johnson, *Owning Your Own Shadow,* 102, 111.

9. P. Block, *The Trustee Educator,* vol. 2, no. 2 (Indianapolis, Ind.: Trustee Leadership Development, 1991), 1, 4, 6.

10. H. Owen, *Leadership Is* (Potomac, Md.: Abbott Publishing, 1980), 85.

11. M. S. Peck, *People of the Lie: The Hope for Healing Human Evil* (New York: Simon & Schuster, 1983), 221.

12. Carl Jung defines the shadow as "the negative side of personality, the sum of all those unpleasant qualities we like to hide, together with insufficiently developed functions and the content of the personal unconscious." Quoted in *Meeting the Shadow,* eds. Connie Zweig and Jeremiah Abrams (New York: St. Martins, 1991), 3.

13. P. J. Palmer, *The Company of Strangers: Christians and the Renewal of America's Public Life* (New York: Crossroad Publishing, 1990), 30.

14. Trustee Leadership Development (TLD) is a national leadership education program whose mission is to build the capacity of not-for-profit organizations to serve and to lead. Its origins are rooted in the Lilly Endowment's long-standing interest in and commitment to trusteeship and leadership in the not-for-profit sector. TLD's focus is on the leadership responsible for the governance of these institutions—boards and key executive staff. See Trustee Leadership Development, *Individual and Community Trusteeship* and *Trustee Education Manual* (Indi-

anapolis, Ind.: Trustee Leadership Development, 1991).

15. R. Lynn, "Penetrating the Mystery of Leadership Through Depth Education," *The 1984 Lilly Endowment Annual Report* (Indianapolis, Ind.: Lilly Endowment, 1984), 8.

16. R. K. Greenleaf, *Servant Leadership: A Journey into the Nature of Legitimate Power and Greatness* (New York: Paulist Press, 1977), 25.

17. Lynn, "Penetrating the Mystery," 8.

18. Palmer, *To Know As We Are Known,* 11.

5

Spirited Connections

Learning to Tap
the Spiritual Resources
in Our Lives and Work

D. Susan Wisely
Elizabeth M. Lynn

*T*he theme of this anthology—spirituality, leadership, and the workplace—creates a contradiction, an unholy trinity of sorts. In our culture we tend to think of spirituality and organizational life as mutually exclusive, even hostile to one another. The spiritual journey is imagined as an interior movement, carrying us inward, upward, or downward but not outward into our relationships with others, and especially not into our working relationships. Spiritual life is considered a private matter and one's work life a messy public necessity, distracting at best, spiritually desiccating at worst.

Recently, thoughtful people in a variety of fields have begun to attend to questions of spirituality in the context of organizational life. Even in these efforts, however, the presumption persists that organizational life is fundamentally inhospitable to spiritual life. For example, a recent workshop entitled "Spiritual Practice and Organizational Life" offers participants tips on "developing a spiritual life within the modern secular context of living and working." Its organizers promise to guide us onto "a path of interior development throughout the organizational contexts in which most of us move" and to help us "take a standpoint that is separate from the organization's expectations."[1] In this line of thinking, an organization is at best a neutral setting for our personal spiritual pursuits and at worst a hostile one, which we must actively strive to offset.

Such presumptions of hostility between spiritual life and organizational life are certainly understandable. After all, the effects of organizational everyday realities upon the human spirit are frequently negative. It is a sad but honest commentary on our ways of relating to one another that a work community, like any other community, can so easily foster feelings of worthlessness and powerlessness in its members.

Still, we believe that organizational life has more to offer than a paycheck and a headache. In uncultivated and largely unrecognized ways, it holds out essential spiritual resources to contemporary culture. Our spirits are nurtured by *living in relation*—in relation to others and to a larger good. But our life in relation to others has been diminished by the structures of modern existence.

Where do we connect with others outside our immediate circle of interest and intrigue? Certainly churches and synagogues offer a crucial arena of connection. And yet (for reasons which we will not explore here), many people today no longer participate in organized religious communities. So too, in the anonymous culture of the large city, but also in the home-and-mall circuit of smaller towns, neighborhood life is more of a fantasy than a reality.

For better or worse, the workplace has become an essential arena for connection to a larger world. How then can we cultivate that arena? How can we help our own institutions, and other organizations as well, to yield that crucial sense of connection to others and to a larger creation?

At the Lilly Endowment, we have been asking this question for some time. The endowment, a private family foundation located in Indianapolis, was established in 1937 for "the promotion and support of religious, educational, or charitable purposes."[2] Over the years, commitments to religion, education, and community development have spurred a more general concern for the renewal of institutions that link individuals to a tradition and to a community—churches, schools, neighborhood groups, and voluntary organizations. In an effort to support the service of these institutions, members of our staff have been trying to understand and further the art of organizational renewal, both through grant-making programs and through a program of leadership education for nonprofit organizations.

Our efforts have taught us, above all, that certain kinds of educational occasions are crucial for helping people tap into the spiritual resources of their life and work together. We think of these occasions as hospitable spaces for disciplined reflection, clearings in which the members of an organization can converse and reflect together within the ongoing context of an organization's life. In such spaces, and through carefully structured encounters between their own stories and larger communal stories or traditions, people can begin to discover what binds them together, beyond an organizational economy of rewards and grievances.

Our attempts to cultivate hospitable spaces for disciplined reflection in organizational life, both for organizations through the leadership education program and also for our own staff through a continuing education program, are relatively recent and unrefined. But we have learned a few things about the art of cultivating these occasions in the past several years and would like to take this opportunity to share our emerging insights. In this chapter, we talk about some of the things we have learned that have been especially effective in revitalizing the spirit of people and their institutions.

For the most part, we suggest specific practices, rather than attempting to generalize from these to a system or philosophy. It is not easy, nor perhaps finally fruitful, to speak abstractly about spiritual life. We encounter the movements of spirit indirectly: in odd awakening moments of daily life, in sharing the stories of our lives with one another, in responding to a common history or common text, in listening to our own intuitions, in thinking with imagination. Such encounters do not eventuate in consensus or creed so much as in a changed way of seeing, one that enlarges our sense of a common world.

Our method carries with it certain theological convictions, then. In this chapter, we deliberately avoided articulating a definition of spirit, speaking somewhat vaguely of "something more" that relates us to one another and focusing our attention on manifestations of that "something more" in organizational life. Some people believe that they can give a precise name to spirit; others believe just as firmly that they cannot. Our own sense is that spirit finally cannot be said; it can only be shown. It shows itself in community. It shows itself in conversation—about our own stories, our common history, and our institutional mission. It shows itself in the reading of common texts. It shows itself in the language and wisdom of various religious traditions. And, finally, it shows itself in leaders who are not afraid to become teachers, creating a hospitable space within which people can discover their connections to one another and to a larger creation.

"Connect, only connect," pleads E. M. Forster in his novel *Howard's End,* voicing the first and final demand of the human spirit. Perhaps, by providing hospitable spaces for disciplined reflection, leaders-as-teachers give the members of their working community the permission, the resources, and the language to do just that: to "connect, only connect."

The Power of Community and Conversation

Speaking to the American Association of Higher Education, Parker Palmer offered the following definition of community: "I understand community as a capacity for relatedness within individuals, relatedness not only to people but to events in history, to nature, to the world of ideas, and yes, to things of the spirit."[3] Community, or our capacity for relatedness, is crucial to education. We learn by relating ourselves to a larger reality, one that includes other people but also, in Palmer's image, nature, history, thought, and spirit.

Unfortunately, much of the current work in organizational education tends to subvert this basic condition for good education. Programs for leadership or staff development often focus on individual learners and intentionally remove them from their daily context of relationships, their natural community. Training workshops of this sort, which introduce us to others in our field or position of leadership, have virtues of their own. But they cannot compensate for the unique educative powers of conversation and reflection with our own colleagues and neighbors. These are the people who embody community for us, who provide, and sometimes withhold, the daily nourishment of our spirits, who empower or immobilize us by their very presence in our lives. And, as Palmer has also observed, a community *always* includes the people we wish would go away. "Community," he has said, "is that place where the person you least want to live with always lives."[4]

In organizational life, acknowledging the spiritual necessity of community means clearing hospitable spaces within our ordinary work situations, where we can enter into regular conversation with our own colleagues. By *conversation,* we mean something akin to the practice of *dialogue,* as explicated by management thinker Peter Senge in his book on learning organizations, *The Fifth Discipline.* "Team learning starts with 'dialogue,'" he writes, "the capacity of members of a team to suspend assumptions and enter into a genuine 'thinking together.' To the Greeks *dia-logos* meant a free-flowing of meaning through a group, allowing the group to discover insights not attainable individually." Senge contrasts the communal consensuality of dialogue to the competitive ethos of *discussion,* which, as he says, "has its roots in 'percussion' and 'concussion,' literally a heaving of ideas back and forth in a winner-take-all competition."[5] As we all know, discussion of the sort Senge describes is a commonplace of organizational life. Opportunities for dialogue, on the other hand, are much more rare and must be gently cultivated.

Intriguingly, our own work in leadership education suggests that the practice of storytelling, particularly the telling of personal stories, can create conditions of openness where more formal procedural efforts have failed. Why is it that in sharing stories we truly open ourselves to the experience of others? Why, in "getting personal," do we seem more able to "go public," more able to transcend ourselves and acknowledge a common humanity with others? One reason for this paradox may have to do with the convention of speaking and listening that traditionally accompany the telling of stories in our culture. A storyteller implicitly expects from his or her audience that "suspension of disbelief" which, in the famous words of Samuel Taylor Coleridge, "constitutes poetic faith."[6] By suspending disbelief, if only for the moment, we assume an unusual openness to the veracity and perceptions of others: we listen and attend, instead of merely awaiting our opportunity to challenge the speaker. A special kind of space opens up, and in that space the teller of the story is free to decide where the narrative begins and ends, what is included and what is left out, and what the relevant facts and feelings are. The climate thus created allows people to make connections between their experiences and to discover their common humanity in new ways, at deeper levels. Storytelling is one of the few naturally occurring occasions where our society supports dialogue in preference to discussion.

In the telling of stories, paradoxically, the personal becomes a pathway to the communal. Moreover, we have found that personal accounts of human frailty or failure are especially successful as a means of encouraging a sense of connection or common humanity. This

107

finding may at first seem to contradict the advice of those who have studied effective leaders. In their influential book *Leaders,* Warren Bennis and Burt Nanus coin the phrase "the Wallenda factor" to draw attention to the way leaders respond to failure. "These leaders put all their energies into their task. They don't even think about failure," Bennis and Nanus contend, "don't even use the word, relying on such synonyms as 'mistake,' 'glitch,' 'bungle,' or countless others. . . . Never *failure*."[7] The message seems to be: To contemplate failure, much less confess it, inhibits a leader's effectiveness. Error, on the other hand, is acceptable, as Bennis maintains elsewhere. "Leaders embrace error. [They] are not afraid to make mistakes, and admit them when they do."[8] The leader's capacity to admit mistakes is seen as essential to creating an environment where risk taking is encouraged and where learning is possible.

What important insight lies behind this distinction between "failure" and its synonyms? Bennis and Nanus give us a clue: "For a lot of people, the word 'failure' carries with it a finality, the absence of movement characteristic of a dead thing, to which the automatic human reaction is helpless discouragement. But for the successful leader, failure is a beginning, the springboard of hope."[9]

What allows people to view failure as a beginning rather than an end? In our experience, the "springboard of hope" is the clear and certain possibility of forgiveness. We learn of this possibility through our religious traditions; we experience its power through forgiving

108

and being forgiven. More than a simple shift of words is needed to give ourselves and others permission to risk failure. We need to name and honor the experience of forgiveness. When we share stories of failure and forgiveness, we discover how closely our sense of personal worth is linked to community. We gain hope from longer traditions that remind us of our limits and teach us the practices of reconciliation. Under appropriate circumstances, public admission of failure can lead a community into acknowledgments of its shared humanity, maybe even an experience of grace.

On the other hand, personal sharing, especially of perceived injuries and insults in the workplace, easily degenerates into a group gripe for so many "victims." Conversations of this kind may be therapeutic, but they often fall short of being educational—which is to say, they run the risk of consoling without teaching. Whereas therapy (appropriately, for its purposes) turns us back on our own story, education opens our eyes to a larger context for that story. In relating our experiences to that larger context, we may also begin to perceive that our relation to one another extends beyond the tasks of the moment or the psychological economy of the workplace: that we have something called "spirit" in common.

There are many ways to gain access to that larger context. In higher education, as Parker Palmer has persuasively argued, what is being taught—the subject—can be a steadying reference point for the community of truth. In organizational life, two equally useful standards or reference points are the mission and history of an institution. Indeed, our own experience indicates that intentional efforts to understand the institution's mission and history can help people relate their own efforts and stories to something beyond themselves. In our leadership education efforts during the past decade, we have encouraged various approaches to communal reflection on the history and mission of an institution. We have found that regular opportunities for reflecting together are essential, if people are to understand their institution's particular place and potential for service within the larger society.

Taking Time to Consider Mission

Convictions about the value of "mission-talk" are, of course, far from new. Good leaders have long understood, at least intuitively, that clarity about mission is the spiritual core of an institution. But, perhaps because mission-talk borders on a cliché, fresh ideas about how to encourage productive consideration of mission are few and far between. We all know that reflection on mission can be superficial, amounting to little more than a rote reiteration of the organizational charter or a trendy translation of its terms into the values of the day. But mission-talk can also go surprisingly deep. What, one might ask, makes it a superficial or significant group exercise?

A story from our own grant-making files suggests some answers to this question. Five years ago, the Lilly Endowment made grants to eleven national nonprofit organizations. Each grant was $30,000, and each came with an important proviso: The grant was to be used not to finance program activities but to free leaders to think historically about their institution's purpose and how it could renew its service in a changing world.

The groups we contacted responded with as much skepticism as appreciation. The reaction of Peggy Charren, founder and executive director of Action for Children's Television (ACT), was typical. "When I first heard about it," says Charren, "I thought, 'Gee, I do that all the time.' I mean, if I didn't figure out how to run ACT, it would be running into the ground. Every time I do something I think about whether it's the right thing to do. But it was $30,000 and I suppose I could always think about it better, right?"[10]

Charren chose to "do it better" by expanding both her conversation circle and the context for her considerations of purpose. First of all, she used the extra money and the leverage of a foundation mandate to enlist staff members, trustees, ACT supporters, and other advocacy groups in her reflections. Second, she enlarged the focus of those reflections beyond the future of ACT itself, to the future of children's television.

An unusual decision resulted from this process of consultation and reflection. Charren and other ACT leaders concluded that, with the passage of the Children's Television Act of 1990, ACT's national advocacy mission had in fact been accomplished. They decided that, after twenty-four years of service, ACT should go out of business in a responsible way, using its remaining resources both to help other groups ensure the effectiveness of standing legislation and to fund a lecture series and graduate research program on children and the media at Harvard's School of Education.

The decision to close ACT testified, of course, to the character of Charren's leadership. As Jeffrey A. Sonnenfeld, director of Emory University's Center for Leadership and Career Studies, told *The Chronicle of Philanthropy,* "It takes a tremendous amount of self-confidence to say that a group's mission is complete. By Peggy Charren's decision to leave the scene, she showed that the cause is greater than the institution or her own personal involvement, that she's not concerned about her own heroic stature."[11] And yet, as Sonnenfeld's own words imply, Charren's leadership had communal as well as personal sources. She derived great strength from her ties to a community of fellow advocates for high-quality children's television.

The story of ACT teaches us several things about what carries a consideration of mission beyond the development of a new corporate slogan. First, as Charren herself stressed, she was impelled to a new way of thinking both by a foundation mandate and by the allocation of resources specifically for reflection and consultation about mission. Foundation resources may not always be available, but an organization can be inspired as much (indeed, probably more) by similar actions on the part of its own board of directors. Second, reflection on mission can benefit from a new and larger configuration of conversation partners, including not just the usual administrators and staff but trustees and even members of one's own public. Finally, people can be moved in self-transcending ways by attention to the larger context, attention unclouded by concerns about the organization's own sense of identity.

This final point—the importance of that larger context—deserves a little further exploration. Much contemporary work on organizational development attests to the power of a larger context or story. For example, Peter Senge tells us, "Most of the leaders with whom I have worked agree that the first leadership design task concerns developing vision, values, purpose or mission." He goes on to report "a surprising discovery":

> Although the three leaders with whom I talked operate in completely different industries . . . and although the specifics of their views differed substantially, they each appeared to draw their own inspiration from the same source. Each perceived a deep story and sense of purpose that lay behind his vision, what we have come to call the *purpose story*—a larger "pattern of becoming" that gives unique meaning to his personal aspirations and his hopes for their organization. . . .
>
> I began to see that these leaders were doing something different from just "story-telling," in the sense of using stories to teach lessons or transmit bits of wisdom. They were relating *the* story—the overarching explanation of why they do what they do, how their organization needs to evolve, and how that evolution is part of something larger. As I re-

113

flected back on gifted leaders whom I have known, I realized that this "larger story" was common to them all, and conversely that many otherwise competent managers in leadership positions were not leaders of the same ilk precisely because they saw no larger story.[12]

Senge's observations are true to our own experience of the importance of a larger story or context. But where do these "purpose stories" come from? According to Senge, "The purpose stories of the three leaders above each describes a context of deep issues that transcend the problems of any one organization, implies a sense of urgency that makes action imperative, and illuminates *their own personal vision*."[13] This seems to imply that the purpose story is rooted in personal vision, in the insights, experiences, and intuitions of these leaders as individuals. But we have found that there are powerful communal sources of the purpose story, as well—sources to be discovered in corporate reflection on the history of an organization.

Exploring History

As a quick glance at any popular periodical will reveal, American adults are deeply concerned today about the geographical and historical ignorance and isolationism of our young people. But we fail to see how our own historical ignorance is isolating us from one another—in the workplace as much as in the nation or world. For better or worse, people within a particular organization or profession are united by more than the circumstances of the moment; they share, and are shaped by, a hidden history of hopes, achievements, failures, and external events. If explored and articulated in a communal process, that hidden history has remarkable power to bind people together in the present. By learning about the ancestry of their current endeavors, staff and trustees can observe how previous members of their organization coped well (or not so well) with serious challenges in another time. They can perceive their own institution as part of a constellation of institutions serving a larger purpose. Most important, they can transcend the episodes of the moment and enter actively into a story that is much larger than themselves.

The experience of the Family Service Association of Indianapolis offers a good example of the ways in which historical study can revitalize an organization. Through a group examination of its 150-year history, the trustees of this organization gained several significant insights into the identity of their institution. First of all, they discovered that they share common roots with a variety of other service organizations in Indianapolis (their own parent organization, the Indianapolis Benevolent Society, had given birth over the years to the Legal Aid Society, the State Board of Charities, the Indiana University School of Social Work, the Indianapolis Children's Bureau, and the Indianapolis Community Chest, which later became the local United Way). By tracing out that "family tree," the board was better able to define what the Family Service Association has in common with other local organizations as well as what has historically distinguished it.

Furthermore, the study process helped to clarify continuities in the agency's own mission and identity. In recent years, the association had begun to provide home-care services to elderly persons without an available family member to help, a move that some trustees felt could not be justified as a form of "family service." By going back into the agency's history, however, the trustees came to see that the terms *family* and *service* had in fact been redefined many times in the course of the agency's existence, in response to profound societal changes. Board members realized that it had been possible to be flexible and at the same time to retain a firm sense of mission and identity. These discoveries infused the leadership of the Family Service Association with renewed confidence and conviction: shortly thereafter, the agency launched several new service programs for the elderly and for young persons with AIDS-related disabilities, with full board support. And the agency also chose *not* to accept a substantial government contract, a decision that trustees attributed to increased clarity about agency standards for adequate care.

In order to help organizations like the Family Service Association discover their own history, several of our grantees have developed a teaching aid called a timeline. This timeline is nothing more, really, than a line on paper, marked off to represent a span of years. On it, members of a group can plot the intersecting trajectories of personal history and shared memory—the history of their organization, region, or field. By helping people see their own stories in relation to a larger story, this simple tool has made a tremendous difference in the spirit and vitality of many organizations. Indeed, evaluation studies of our work in leadership education have gone so far as to suggest that use of the timeline alone can be extremely helpful in clarifying a sense of organizational identity.

In one of our leadership education projects, Trustee Leadership Development (described in more detail in Chapter Four), project leaders have made extensive use of the timeline and have developed an educational process to accompany it. When working with the trustees of a youth leadership program, for instance, the educator had them prepare a timeline recording significant people in the program, program changes, and so forth. According to the director of that program, the board's attempt to articulate its common history initially felt out of control, but it also marked a moment when the group finally began to develop ownership of the program—a moment, in her words, when "individual knowledge" truly became "group knowledge." One result of that sense of shared ownership was a changed relation between the board and staff. The director reported that the educational experience transformed what had really been a group of advisers for her into a board of directors willing to shoulder responsibility for the organization. Board members, in turn, achieved a clearer sense of priorities for future work and a greater understanding of the partnerships the program would need to develop if it wished to accomplish its goals. As a result of this increased clarity about both priorities and partners, the program leaders soon decided to leave the auspices of one educational institution and to seek affiliation with another whose priorities more closely matched their own.

In another trustee education effort employing a timeline, participants were trustees of a community center that had long been a mainstay for African-Americans in the center's hometown. After board members had filled out a timeline charting their organization's history, the facilitator pointed out an eight-year gap in the events recorded. "What happened here?" she asked. What had happened in those eight years, it turned out, was a prolonged crisis over racial issues, in the context of a larger movement for black nationalism. The facilitator's simple question surfaced some longstanding disagreements about the mission of the center—specifically, whether the community to be served should be defined racially (as the black community) or geographically (as the neighborhood surrounding the center). The group acknowledged that they had not dealt productively with these issues at the time, and that although the center had technically survived a crisis during that period, tensions had persisted. By seeing their eight-year struggle in the context of the national civil rights movement, board members were able to work through their feelings and, in time, to agree on future priorities for their struggling organization. The proof of the pudding, as they said, was that, when a minor crisis arose several months later, they trusted one another enough to get through it together.

The lessons of history are not always comfortable. But if those lessons are uncovered and articulated communally (*not* handed down from above as the institution's "tradition"), people can feel empowered by even the most painful discoveries. In the process of defining a common history, individual knowledge can become group knowledge, something that brings people together rather than pulling them apart. Much the same can be said of another simple educational practice: the practice of reading together.

Reading Together

As British novelist and philosopher Iris Murdoch has observed, one of the ways in which we come to understand one another is by talking about a common object. "Use of words by persons grouped around a common object is a central and vital human activity," she writes. "Human beings are obscure to each other, . . . unless they are mutual objects of attention or have common objects of attention."[14] A text can serve as just such "a common object of attention," inviting us to articulate to one another the ways we make sense of the world the text presents to us. In our articulations and construals we may not always agree, but we may be more able to tolerate and accept disagreements of the most fundamental sort when they are provoked, not by work situations, but by responses to a third voice, the voice of the text.

Many of the leadership education programs funded by the Lilly Endowment have attempted to encourage the practice of reading together in organizational life. But perhaps our most valuable experience here has been at home, in our own continuing education program for our staff. Since 1989, people from all positions and divisions of the foundation have been meeting in small groups to discuss a variety of books. There are many possible texts for these encounters. Reading fiction is one possibility, inviting participants to reflect on the "truth" of an imagined world. Or a group may read non-fiction works that encourage conversation about some of the troubling divisions of contemporary life, divisions we all find difficult to discuss. For example, Taylor Branch's *Parting the Waters: America in the King Years* spurred a significant conversation about racial conflict in America. A recent discussion of Jonathan Kozol's study of American schools, *Savage Inequalities,* and Alex Kotlowitz's account of growing up in the inner city, *There Are No Children Here,* was also provocative and illuminating. In addition, we have made use of histories that help staff discover some common contexts and traditions for their work. For instance, as a backdrop to our work in education, we read selections from Lawrence Cremin's well-written and accessible history of American education.[15] Cremin's account of the vast array of institutions and other structures that have contributed to the education of the American people helped our staff understand that "education" is not simply synonymous with "schooling"; that, in fact, each of our foundation's three divisions (community development, religion, and education) can contribute to the education of our citizens, by mobilizing a variety of groups around a common concern like literacy.

Last but not least, a reading group can be an appropriate place for people to rediscover a set of resources that have been effectively exiled from the American workplace: namely, the resources of religious thought and language, as embodied in diverse religious traditions and texts. As a society, we have long held that religion has no place in the secular world of work. And yet we are continually tested in that world of work—not just as workers but as human beings who, in living in relation to one another, are profoundly prone to feelings of worthlessness, envy, and resentment. The insights of popular psychology and organizational culture can, to some extent, help us meet these crises of the spirit. But we have also found that traditional religious concepts like finitude, hope, forgiveness, sin, and grace address a depth of human experience untouched by modern social-scientific terminologies. Religious traditions of all varieties tell us something we do not hear anywhere else in contemporary culture: that our lives and efforts are limited, not just by other people but by something far beyond human constructions of meaning and human obstructions of freedom. And, paradoxically, that experience of limits can free us to be more critical of ourselves and our institutions. In contrast to popular psychology, with its ethos of self-esteem and improvement, a religious perspective can help people relearn the arts of confession and repentance.

In *The Fifth Discipline*, Peter Senge also attempts

121

to reintroduce certain religious dimensions and concepts into organizational life. According to Senge, members of real learning organizations often "talk about being part of something larger than themselves, of being connected, of being generative." In so doing, he suggests, they are trying to describe what the Greeks called *metanoia*—a conversion of sorts, "a fundamental shift or change, or more literally transcendence." Paradoxically, this experience of transcendence helps us to take responsibility for our own lives: we shift "from seeing ourselves as separate from the world to connected to the world, from seeing problems as caused by someone or something 'out there' to seeing how our own actions create the problems we experience."[16]

Perhaps Senge is speaking here of the same sort of disclosive experience we have been describing, with its attendant effects of freeing us to act and helping us to take responsibility for our actions. And yet, significantly, when anchoring his thought in a tradition, Senge eschews living religious vocabularies in favor of the terms of a safely dead and distant civic culture: Greece. In doing so, he reflects a contemporary climate that is increasingly intrigued by the possibilities of religious thought and language and yet is uncomfortable, for various reasons, with its own varied religious traditions and resources. Perhaps we can overcome some of that discomfort, and help ourselves and others to rediscover and reappropriate the powers of our own religious traditions, through the simple practice of reading together. By talking with each other about the claims of religious (or philosophical) texts, we can begin to tap into the veins of wisdom running through many different such traditions—our own as well as those that are more safely strange or distant.

In a sense, of course, what we have been advocating here is nothing more than the revival of a few traditional educational practices that have been steadily undermined by modern habits of life. One such practice is the telling of stories; another is the recounting of a common history; and a third is the endangered art of reading together. Educational occasions arranged around these simple practices can enable the members of an organization to discover their deeper relations to one another, especially if such occasions are guided by an able teacher. And that, as we shall see, is where the leader can make a real difference in the spirit of an organization.

The Leader as Teacher

Earlier we referred to the "unholy trinity" created by the terms of this volume—spirituality, leadership, and the workplace. Until now, we have focused almost exclusively on the troubled yet rich relationship between spirituality and the workplace. But what of the third term in that trinity, *leadership?* What place, if any, does leadership have in the practices we have outlined here?

The leader plays many roles in this culture: expert, hero, charismatic, manager, even therapist. As important as these roles may be to the smooth running of society and psyche, however, none of them has much to

123

do with the kind of community and conversation we have been advocating. Instead, quite obviously, the leader who would create educational occasions must be a teacher, one who, in Parker Palmer's definition, creates "a space in which the community of truth is practiced."[17]

In contrast to other leadership roles (in which the leader possesses something others lack, be it charisma or character, knowledge or technical expertise), the leader-as-teacher does not necessarily know more than anyone else. Instead, he or she helps others to discover what they, in some sense, already know. "We are wiser than we know," Ralph Waldo Emerson once said. "If we will not interfere with our thought . . . we know the particular thing and every thing and every man."[18] The kind of knowledge Emerson is speaking of here—an intuitive knowledge of "every thing and every man"—is not a knowledge we attain to individually: it is in us as creatures of this world, that is, by living in relation to one another and to a larger reality. We learn what it is that we most deeply believe (and test those beliefs crucially against the perspectives of others) through a continual process of conversation, reflection, and action in the world.

The leader, then, is one who can create occasions for that process of reflection, conversation, and renewed action. But what enables someone to create these occasions? What makes someone a good teacher of this kind? The teacher's most important attribute, we believe, is a capacity to bring diverse perspectives into relation with one another and to elicit patterns of meaning among those perspectives. He or she helps people to make connections with one another and, just as important, to make corrections in their own ways of seeing, when challenged by the power of the larger community or context.

One popular way of putting this is to say that the leader-as-teacher helps us discover "common ground."[19] But the common ground of "spirit" is not simply the lowest common denominator in our separate ways of seeing. It is something more invisible, experiential, not directly describable—a set of connections implicitly ordering our common world. Another way of describing the process of making connections is to say that people must learn to see from one another's perspectives. As the old cliché puts it, "You can't criticize somebody until you have walked a mile in their moccasins." This popular expression suggests that the challenge is to move over into someone else's shoes in order to see things their way. The implication is that we live in different worlds or realities, like so many self-enclosed bubbles circling through the atmosphere.

Attempting to view things from someone else's perspective is an important exercise, if only because it teaches a certain modesty about our own perspective. Still, we want to say that the task of relating to one another is more complicated than such an exercise would suggest, with its vision of multiple worlds. For, after all, we finally live in *one world,* a world that somehow, mysteriously, accommodates both ourselves and others. The spiritual challenge, then, is to enlarge our own way of seeing to include that other person, not to hop worlds but to see our separate worlds as one. This takes a searching process of conversation and description: we must describe what we see in such a way that the other person finally recognizes it as part of his or her own world. In this way that other perspective is not simply tolerated, it is *inspirited,* made vital and alive.

Above all, a teacher can aid in this process of description and mutual recognition by using imagination: by finding symbols, analogies, allegories, and other stories that help people describe their vision to one another indirectly. To be an imaginative teacher, one need not be blessed with a special muse, just an open and analogizing mind. Let us offer one homely example from our own experience. Several years ago, we wrote an essay called "Invitation to Reflection" for members of the endowment's Religion Division; it was designed to help them discuss the shape and spirit of their grant-making program during a staff retreat. In order to facilitate conversation about the "spirit" animating their work, we deliberately shifted from speaking of grant-making programs to a geographical analogy, in which grants create a "terrain of service" in the world. Lists of grants provide a topographical description of that terrain, we suggested, and, like all topographical descriptions, they have their uses. They provide a map of sorts, helping us move through a particular landscape.

Yet a map does not satisfy the question, "What is America?" One still wants a description of the kind of life lived within these boundaries and these structures. So too, a list of grants, even one supplemented by tangible goals and results, does not satisfy the question, "What does the Religion Division do?" We have to ask, in addition, what kind of life do these grants serve? Imagine the work of the Religion Division as a terrain of service: it has boundaries which limit the reach of its service and, within those boundaries, definite structures which foster a certain form of human life, embodied in particular activities and imbued with a particular spirit. How would you describe that form of life? What are its quintessential activities? What is the spirit that animates it?[20]

By imagining their work as a terrain with specific structures and activities, members of the staff were able to move beyond the difficulties we all have in articulating the spiritual dimensions of everyday work like grant making. This map exercise is a simple example of the power of analogy, one of many possible imaginative tools a teacher can use to help others comprehend truths that can be approached only indirectly.

The art of making connections, as a leader, sometimes means accepting that you cannot understand that other perspective. It means allowing other people their truth and action, even if those do not make sense to you. But again, the capacity to accept (and to forgive) is found not so much in the isolated individual as in the lived community: for it requires faith in a larger reality binding us all together. In the words of theologian Reinhold Niebuhr, "Nothing that is worth doing can be achieved in our lifetime; therefore we must be saved by hope. Nothing which is true or beautiful or good makes complete sense in any immediate context of history; therefore we must be saved by faith. Nothing we do, however virtuous, can be accomplished alone; therefore we are saved by love. No virtuous act is quite as virtuous from the standpoint of our friend or foe as it is from our standpoint. Therefore we must be saved by the final form of love which is forgiveness."[21]

In Conclusion

The activities we have been advocating in this essay may strike the reader as an odd mix of the obvious and the impossible. On the one hand, the practices of conversation, storytelling, historical inquiry, and reading together are age-old basic learning techniques. On the other hand, all of these practices require time, space, and a capacity for personal disclosure—requirements that run counter to the dominant ethos of organizational life, with its anxieties about efficiency and professional comportment.

Indeed, when the Lilly Endowment began to encourage these practices in what we have called a "depth approach" to leadership education, we assumed that our programs would have limited appeal. We knew that the various practices of "depth reflection" took more time and imposed a more intentional, disciplined educational process than most organizations either expect or have experienced. Our staff was truly surprised, therefore, by the degree of enthusiasm for reflection of this kind and the extent of demand from a wide variety of groups.

Perhaps one clue to the unexpected popularity of a so-called depth approach lies precisely in what some have called its unusual "spiritual dimension." According to the testimony of participants, educational occasions of the sort we have described here give people a rare chance to talk with each other about the deeper significance of their organization in their own lives and for the larger society. Furthermore, by inquiring together into their mission and history, or by attending to a common text of religion, literature, or philosophy, they may be enabled to speak about what matters to them in older, half-forgotten, but more powerful ways than those offered by the technical language of "organizational development" or "strategic planning" or "sound management."

Finally, our experience makes us wonder about the persistent power of common inquiry and reflection, not simply for working communities but for the larger human community. Could it be that educational occasions of the sort we have been describing are rare public opportunities for moral and religious discourse, or, in other language, conversation about varying perspectives on questions of ultimate concern? If organizations begin to discover the power of this kind of conversation in their own internal deliberations, can they also find ways to encourage a wider conversation of this sort as part of their service to the broader society?

Notes

1. Central Indiana Friends of C. G. Jung, "Spiritual Practice and Organizational Life Workshop" (Indianapolis, Ind.: Central Indiana Friends of Jung, Oct. 1992), 1.

2. *Lilly Endowment Inc. Annual Report for 1950* (Indianapolis, Ind.: Lilly Endowment, 1950), 2.

3. P. Palmer, "Community, Conflict and Ways of Knowing," *Change Magazine, 19* (Sept./Oct. 1987): 24.

4. Palmer, "Community, Conflict . . . ," 20.

5. P. Senge, *The Fifth Discipline* (New York: Doubleday Currency, 1990), 10.

6. J. J. Jackson (ed.), "Biographia Literaria," in *Samuel Taylor Coleridge* (Oxford: Oxford University Press, 1985), 314.

7. W. Bennis and B. Nanus, *Leaders: The Strategies for Taking Charge* (New York: Harper & Row, 1985), 69.

8. W. Bennis, *On Becoming a Leader* (Reading, Pa.: Addison-Wesley, 1989), 194.

9. Bennis and Nanus, *Leaders,* 71.

10. J. Moore, "Peggy Charren's Closing ACT," *The Chronicle of Philanthropy* (July 28, 1992): 25.

11. Moore, "Peggy Charren," 26.

12. Senge, *Fifth Discipline,* 343, 345–346.

13. Senge, *Fifth Discipline,* 345–346 (emphasis added).

14. I. Murdoch, *The Sovereignty of Good* (London: Ark Paperbacks, 1985), 32–33.

15. See L. A. Cremin, *American Education: The Metropolitan Experience 1876–1980* (New York: Harper & Row, 1988).
16. Senge, *Fifth Discipline,* 13.
17. P. J. Palmer, "Good Teaching," *Change Magazine* (Jan./Feb. 1990): 12.
18. S. E. Whicher, R. Spiller, and W. E. Williams (eds.), *The Early Lectures of Ralph Waldo Emerson* (Cambridge, Mass.: Harvard University Press, 1959–1972), vol. 3, p. 42.
19. Peter Senge speaks of the value of a consensus built "from the 'content' of our individual views—discovering what part of my view is shared by you and the others." This, he explains, "is our 'common ground,' upon which we can all agree" (*Fifth Discipline,* 248).
20. D. S. Wisely and E. M. Lynn, "Invitation to Reflection" (Unpublished paper, May 1987), 3.
21. R. Niebuhr, *The Irony of American History* (New York: Scribner, 1952), 63.

6

Partnering with God
Ignatian Spirituality
and Leadership in Groups

Brian O. McDermott, S.J.

*I*n this chapter I want to explore, in a preliminary way, some of the connections between one stream of Roman Catholic spirituality, namely, the spirituality of St. Ignatius of Loyola, and the role of authority in the life of groups and organizations. I see myself involved in the enterprise of bridge building, developing the bridge from the theology/spirituality side of the river, moving toward the social science side. I am writing this out of the conviction that there are resources in Western Christian traditions of spirituality that are available for those seeking to explore the spiritual dimensions of group and organizational life but who may be put off by some of the doctrinal aspects of Western Christianity (such as Roman Catholicism). Sometimes Westerners look to the East for spiritual wisdom and overlook a rich and complex tradition in the West.

Some Catholic Christian Convictions About Spirituality

The infinite mystery we call God acts in concrete human history. When the New Testament refers to the kingdom or reign of God, it is referring to God's work or project of leading all creation to its fulfillment in the depths of God, a fulfillment that entails the transformation of the material, psychical, and spiritual world in its unity and diversity. Acting in accord with God's project requires people to engage the world, including the problems and potentials of public life.

God, the infinite, incomprehensible mystery, creates human beings so that God can give God's self away to them as their full actualization. God then invites humans to partner with God in the divine project: freely to participate in the processes of creativity, reconciliation, and transformation that are the most basic dimensions of the project. When a person chooses a career in public life out of a desire to foster the common good, such a desire can be interpreted in a Christian way as an implicit desire to participate in God's project in the world.

Christians believe that God gives God's self away to humans in a twofold way that is ultimately one:

through the inner world of our human wondering and desiring, thinking and planning, and the outer world of nature and human history. The divine depth of the inner gift is God's Holy Spirit; the focus of God's encounter with us in the external world is Jesus of Nazareth and the community gathered in his name. God shares God's life with us in the fundamental ways that we are structured as human beings: as persons with an inner life and an outer life that together constitute our one human life. Signs of God's work in our world can be found both in our deepest longings, and in the outer events that surround us, insofar as those outer events express fundamental human desires for truth and love.

Practical Spirituality

The preceding paragraphs express an encapsulated theology, an effort to summarize an immense amount of theological thought. What does this theology have to do with practical spirituality? For one thing, it means that God offers God's self to be noticed and responded to both in the external world that surrounds us and the inner world of our psychological life.

Let's begin with the inner life. We are people who wonder and who desire. The deeper we go as wonderers and desirers, the more our wonder and desire have a kind of infinity to them, an unboundedness. These wonders and desires are human, they are finite (not-God). But Christians believe that this wonder and desire, if deep and expressive of our authentic self, are inspired by and filled by the Holy Spirit of God. This Spirit is leading that wonder and desire into the truly infinite life of God and leading us as well to our neighbor in both appreciation and benevolence, the two faces of love.

Let me relate this to the life of a group or organization. There are times when a member of a group, whether a person with formal authority or not, moves from the dance floor of activity in a group to the balcony of reflective, reverent wonder about what is going on in the life of the group. At those times, I believe, the Holy Spirit of God is at work in that person.[1] The human wondering is not identical with God's Spirit, but that Spirit is present in the deeper, "more" involved in that wondering.

Wonder itself is an open-handed, reverential posture. When we wonder at something we simply let it be and savor it for what it is. There are appropriate times to calculate and to manage. But wonder is neither calculation nor management, rather it is the fecund source of all our best thinking, hypothesizing, imagining. Like anything human, wonder can be misused; what flows from it can be turned to destructive uses. But wonder of itself has something childlike about it, even in the most sophisticated observer.

Have you ever wondered at a co-worker who is so caught up in the effort to solve a significant problem that she has moved beyond simply doing her job and is experiencing an intellectual joy in the insights she is getting? She is giving you a glimpse of spirit, of the mind's desire to know, which can have a kind of joy associated with it.

Desire also has a mysterious dimension to it. We can desire all manner of things: a new car, sexual satisfaction, a change in our relationship with a friend, justice in a corrupt organization, and so forth. Some of our desires express our addictive, fragmented, or unfree self. Other desires express our core humanity as spirit-in-the-world, that is, as seekers of more and more truth and love.[2] These "desires from our center" reflect the true self. We desire truth and love at the deepest level of our humanness; this twofold but at root unitary desire is more who we are as humans than what we have. These desires are bound up with our being human. While some major spiritual traditions would assert that all desires are illusory and enslaving, Christianity believes that our deepest longing for truth, justice, love, and authentic peace are of God, and trustworthy.

Suppose I have been assigned to a task force that is going to be spending long hours on a project that is crucial for the survival of the firm. We will have to start trusting each other if we are to get anywhere with the project. I discover within myself a strong desire to take the risk of sharing a part of myself to help the group become more trustworthy. Such a desire is fully human. But Christians would suggest that such authentic desires like this one are intertwined with the Holy Spirit of God, who creates this desire and seeks to lead it into God's project.

If, at the next meeting of the task force, I experience the desire to hold back, because of fear of losing my identity in sharing too much of myself, the Holy Spirit is present in that desire as well.[3] This loss of identity could take the form of a merging of myself with the group, which would prevent me from making my own contribution to the group. Such a merger could make it very difficult, if not impossible, to add a healthily dissenting voice when "group think" might threaten to take over.

It is not the case that one side of the ambivalence is good, the other evil. Indeed, each is connected with a genuine human value. We are genuinely human when we are healthily self-transcendent, but that implies possessing a self that we can share with others. Christians believe that God is present in that ambivalence, not to solve it as though it were simply a technical problem, but to offer companionship in the process and to invite the healthy but painful kind of loss that must be experienced when one enters more deeply into the two wings of the ambivalence.

The Catholic, Christian tradition teaches that three fundamental resources are available for the person who is living in God's favor: faith, love, and hope. These resources ("virtues") are placed in human beings by God's self-communicating love.

Faith has been defined as a judgment or discernment of value rooted in religious love. Faith is the habit of discerning what is authentically good rather than only apparently good, what is relatively important for one's journey with God and what is secondary or tertiary. As noted author on spirituality Tad Dunne puts it: "To nourish faith is to get into the habit of weighing the value of everything against our felt love for God."[4]

"Love" here refers to our appreciation and benevolence, born of religious love, for known persons or communities. Our being in love with God (a condition brought about by God's grace) begets a love for others that wonders at their goodness (appreciation) and wishes and works for their further flourishing (benevolence). This authentic love for others is, in turn, a sign of authentic love of God. And this love for others is intimately connected to faith. Dunne comments that

> To continue to care for others when our appreciation grows dim, we fall back to faith, the eyes of the heart, which insists on seeing transcendent value even in the dark. Without faith, charity [love] towards the neighbor washes away on the first rainy day. With faith, charity keeps surprising itself on how much self-sacrifice it is willing to endure and towards how many different people it is willing to pour out active, caring love.[5]

Hope is confident desire born of religious love, born of God's love at work in us. We long for and desire the fullest truth and the most complete good, and this unbounded longing is the reflection, in our psyche, of God's drawing us into the future that God wants to bring about with our cooperation. Tad Dunne points out that while faith can often be a matter of cool judgment in difficult times, hope must be borne by affectivity and imagination. "Hope lives on symbols and, thus nourished, can support the judgments of faith."[6] Hope enables us to carry on without certitude about the present.

It gives rather an assurance about the future for those who hope. Hope does not eliminate fear, but it does help us differentiate our fears by distinguishing the fearful darkness of sin and the fearful darkness of divine Mystery.

Faith, love, hope are all gifts of God, yet they look profoundly human when they deploy themselves in our minds and hearts. But because they are gifts, we need to ask for their deepening and not consider them simply achievements on our part. We are called to be healthily dependent on the divine mystery for faith, love, and hope. At the same time, we are supposed to exercise these God-given strengths or virtues in our lives.

Ignatian Spirituality: Key Insights

In the long history of the church, many major spiritual traditions have given specific color and direction to Christian spirituality. The Benedictine, Augustinian, Franciscan, Dominican, Carmelite, and Ignatian are among the better known streams of spirituality. Like the other streams, Ignatian spirituality acquired its full shape within a community of priests and brothers, yet Ignatius was a layman when he first developed his "way." And like the other traditions, Ignatian spirituality was never meant to be the property or practice of only vowed priests, brothers, or nuns; it was intended for laypeople active in secular life.

Ignatius (1491–1556) spent his youthful years as a courtier and soldier in Spain. He underwent a religious conversion after being wounded at the battle of Pamplona in 1521 and became a religious pilgrim. During his university studies, he gathered several people to-gether in a group that in time became a religious order that was meant to be very mobile, not tied down to the traditional devotional practices of religious life (such as chanting the psalms in choir several times a day). He was the first superior general of the Jesuits (Society of Jesus) and for the last sixteen years of his life admin-istered an organization that, before his death, had al-ready spread to many parts of the globe. His spiritual-ity is found in his classic *Spiritual Exercises*[7] (which were intended to help an experienced guide aid other people to seek God's will in their life) and in his autobi-ography, many letters, and the constitutions of the So-ciety of Jesus.[8]

Four of the major insights that form the core of the spirituality of St. Ignatius Loyola are described here and paraphrased in terms of ordinary experience and in relation to the workplace.

1. The Greater Glory of God in Us/Humanity. This phrase expresses Ignatius's conviction that human be-ings exist to increase God's glory "outside of God," that is to say, to foster the authentic flourishing of other hu-mans and of all creation. Ignatius believed that God's inner glory, God's own being, could not increase since it is already infinite. But God's external glory, namely, all creatures, can increase in well-being, and this increase God desires passionately. In other words, we human be-ings have a purpose for living, for acting, for taking responsible risks. We need to lend our creativity and imagination to the project, because what we do or omit

140

is important to what God is trying to bring about in human history. Ignatius saw that a key way of connecting to this purpose was to become aware of our deeper desires for ourselves and our world. There is an endless drive in us for a healthy, nonaddictive, nonconsumerist "more," evidenced by our asking questions and seeking truth and love.

2. *Being Contemplative in Action.* By growing reflectiveness and meditation we dispose ourselves to receive the gift of noticing God in all our actions and being attuned to God's action in each situation. Another way of expressing this is to speak of mindfulness, of learning to live in the present moment, and notice what it is offering us. To follow Ignatius's recommended "examination of consciousness," I would take a few moments at lunchtime and at the end of the day to reflect on the significant events since the last examination, to offer thanks to God for the gifts that came my way in the last few hours, to notice how I was affected by what occurred, what "buttons" in me were pushed, in what ways I felt invited to live out of my true self in fidelity to my deeper, more centered desires. A practice such as this, he believed, could help an individual live more authentically in the here and now of action and busy-ness.

3. *Discipline for the Sake of Interior Freedom: Healthy "Dyings" for the Sake of Greater Life.* Ignatius stressed the need to let go of false parts of ourselves so that more of us might become available to God's purposes in the world. The selfish ego with its narrowmindedness must diminish to allow a more self-transcendent

141

spirit to arise. For example, how many times do we treat our interpretations of what we perceive about others' behavior in the workplace as automatically true, rather than as the hypotheses they really are, hypotheses that require verification? Only if we become freer of our need to prejudge will we be free enough to let an insight or bright idea be a hypothesis, open to reevaluation on the basis of additional data. Underneath this need to prejudge lies a deep-seated anxiety that Ignatius thought could be transformed by increasing our healthy belonging to God, the source of our lives.

4. Guidance in Seeking God's Will (Seeking the Greater Glory of God in Us). As author of *The Spiritual Exercises,* Ignatius offered aids to those seeking to make choices that were consonant with their deepest and best desires and consonant with God's will for them.[9] Psychologist Michael O'Sullivan recently summed up Ignatius's approach in terms of "trusting your feelings and using your head."[10]

Ignatius offered help for distinguishing between "human-friendly" affective movements within us and those movements that were harmful to people if they colluded with them. A lawyer's wish to increase *pro bono* work may spring from her authentic self and may invite a healthy stretching on her part. But a doctor's enthusiastic desire to simplify his lifestyle in a way that ignores his commitments to his wife and children is *prima facie* a deceptive impulse; certainly it needs to be checked out. Even among actions that are really good we need to be able to distinguish which ones we are called to respond to and which not. Our affections repulse what is perceived as dangerous and seek out what appears to be good. It is important then to be able to discern affections or attractions to determine which are orienting us to the values that should have a claim on our attention and energy at this point in our lives. Ignatius believed that a person who was truly free of inordinate attachments could trust his or her affective life, if it were properly discerned.

One of Ignatius's suggestions for seeking God's will in a situation involves several steps. To begin, we must get in touch with the purpose of our life—namely, the greater glory of God in creation—and let that become our orientation. Then we should enter into the significant alternatives (all of which must be moral), get the feel of them through actively imagining what each would be like if it were chosen. The foreseeable consequences of each choice need to be entered into as well. Then we are to choose the alternative that offers the better fit with the purpose of our life. If this does not suffice, we can then imagine giving advice to a friend whose well-being we care about. Which alternative would we advise for our friend? Another way is to imagine being on our deathbed. Looking back from that standpoint, what would we wish we had chosen? This approach, which I have only summarized here, has the advantage of leading a person away from very short-term considerations or from biases that spring from narrow self-interest.

Spirituality and Leadership

I would like to turn now to some examples of the resources that Ignatian spirituality holds out to people who lead organizations from a position of formal authority. In the perspective I use in this chapter, *leadership* and *authority* are not synonyms; they are interrelated but distinct.

Leadership involves mobilizing a group to do its work. The work may be defining the problem, the actual effort to solve the problem, or connecting the group to its larger purposes so that it becomes apparent why it is important to solve the problem. Any individual or subgroup in an organization can exercise leadership in this sense, regardless of official job title. In contrast, people who hold authority in a formal sense were officially appointed to the role, and that role is defined by a job description. These leaders will be charged with making a certain range of executive decisions in relation to the goals and objectives of the organization, will have other people reporting to them, and will be in turn accountable to the expectations of those above them.

But there is something more fundamental involved in the exercise of authority than particular executive decisions. These decisions may well involve very complex and sophisticated matters but they are nonetheless a routine way of dealing with problems. But there is another kind of work, one that involves the tasks of adapting to very new and different situations. The situation calls for a new defining of the challenge or issue, for determining what new learnings are necessary to relate to the challenge, and for doing the new learning—all of which means that those involved are being asked to change. That is why this kind of work has been called transformational.

In the process of transformational work, the person with authority is meant to create—or better, be the principal agent in creating—a "holding environment" for the life and activities of the group or organization. This environment is a psychological space where the leader acts to contain the energies and distresses of the group. The objective is to help people stay with the work that needs to be done despite distracting emotional forces. Transformational work, and the challenge that calls it forth, can introduce tremendous disequilibrium into the life of the group. Anxiety, denial, work avoidance (in the various forms that this can take), and conflict within the work group and with other groups are all fairly predictable. In this situation the authority person represents the boundaries of the group, the within and the without of the group of people. This person also represents the purposes of the group's existence and its expectations about those purposes, becoming in effect the repository for the group's expectations. Soon those expectations can take the form of demanding that the transformational work be turned back into the technical, routine work of problem solving—a maneuver that would be simply evasion of the real challenge before the group.

The levels of expectation placed on the authority

figure are difficult, if not impossible, to chart, especially when the group is swimming in the new waters of transformational challenge. Some of the expectations are conscious, but many of them are unconscious. The individual with authority represents the longing of the group's members to belong to something larger than themselves. A part of their psyche wants to surrender to the authority person, to ally with him or her, as a seemingly direct way to enter more fully into the life of the group. Trusting the authority person is tied up with the possibility of trusting the group.

On the other hand, the individuals' fear of losing themselves or part of themselves in the group is played out in their relationship with the authority figure. That person will have to take the heat from members who act out of their fear for their individuality. There is no way that the authority person can unremittingly respond to the expectations of the group or individuals within the group. Eventually the authority figure will frustrate the group's expectations. Indeed, unless this happens fairly early on the authority risks falling into the syndrome of the "charismatic leader" who uses his or her (perhaps considerable) talents to respond to the expectations, which has the inevitable effect of fueling them. Human beings have infinite expectations, unconsciously if not consciously. We want more and more truth, goodness, acceptance, love. Less admirably, we want more and more ego aggrandizement ("if I don't keep growing—at your expense—I'll die") or more and more safety ("one can never be too safe").

There is no healthy way around it: if the authority

person is gifted and capable of building up informal authority by responding to at least some of the significant expectations of the group, he or she is going to fail in the eyes of the group at some point, because it will be impossible to remain on the upward curve of satisfying expectations. Authority represents purpose, orientation, decision making, boundaries and group definition, safety, challenge, nurturance, and care giving. Yet every human authority is finite, limited, equipped with only so much imagination, intelligence, resourcefulness, and courage. All members of a human group, on some level of their psyche, want it all. We seem to be fashioned for some kind of totality, some wholeness, that keeps showing up in our relationship to authority. We hate it, question it, want it, expect enormous things from it.

This places an extraordinary burden on the person who holds authority over a group. Modern organizations give their leaders many resources to work with, but one area has largely been ignored up to now: the resources inherent in spirituality. These resources hold out the promise of help.

I would like now to explore briefly three aspects of authority in relationship to Ignatian spirituality: the need for partners, the call to disidentify from expectations, and the recognition that the group is larger than the individual members.

The Need for Partners

First of all, the person in authority needs partners. Ordinarily, on the human level, this means consultants from outside the group or (much trickier) friends and allies within the group. But Ignatian spirituality reminds a person that there is another Partner, infinite in life, truth, and love, who is very close and intimate to the person in authority, to the individuals in the group, and to the group as a living entity more than the sum of its parts. The Holy Spirit of God, God's inner word, is active within the authority and the group, drawing the various people in the group into God's project, God's greater glory in us, which will show up again and again in very human terms: more truthfulness, more authentic love, greater and more inclusive justice and compassion. By staying attentive to God's drawing him or her into relationship, the leader will be helped to stay finitely human and not yield to the temptation to play God.

The seductions of a group when its expectations are being met or being frustrated are powerful forces working on the psyche of the authority figure. A story will illustrate this. Alice, the instructor of a course in individual rights and the common good in twentieth-century American political theories, had changed her pedagogy in the middle of a semester. From primarily lecturing, she moved into returning more and more of the work back to the class. Conflicts arose between some of the men and women in the class, as well as between people of different personalities. Some of the male students, having become extremely uncomfortable with the conflicted atmosphere in the classroom, were exasperated even more when Alice tried to point out that the dynamics in the class could be viewed as mirroring some of the topics in the course. One of the students, Joe, made a passionate speech in class, begging Alice to return to her strength—her brilliant lectures.

That night Alice reflected on Joe's remarks. She admitted some self-doubt. Perhaps Joe was right. After all, she had changed the rules in midstream, and that raised the issue of fairness. But she still felt her original reasons for changing were sound.

Alice decided to, as she puts it, "sit before God" with Joe's challenge and the questions going on within her. She sat down in her "reflection chair" in her living room, joined her fingertips, and tried to become quiet. She reminded herself that she was in the presence of God, the invisible, incomprehensible mystery of love. She became aware of her breathing, in and out. She offered the outward breathing to God, letting it represent the turmoil going on within her. She let the breathing in represent her desire that God be with her and within her. She quieted down, not completely but a bit. She let herself imagine herself with Joe as he pointed the finger at her, berating her but also praising her lecturing ability. His imagined remarks distressed her once again, and she let that happen. She breathed in and out, and noticed Joe before her, and gently noticed her own inner response. Soon she had the felt sense—no inner pictures—that God was holding both Joe and herself in God's cupped hands, just as they were: Joe berating and praising her, she receiving what he was saying and noticing the effect of it within her. It was as if God were saying to her: "Joe is feeling unsafe, and you want your students to 'taste' what the common good is when it happens among people. Hold steady, keep at what you are doing, not because you are doing it perfectly, but because you have entered on this path, and good learning might come of it for at least some students, and why are you a teacher, ultimately?"

These words were not said to her; rather this was her articulation, later, of the felt sense that was given to her. The felt sense was not God, it was a product of her benevolent preconscious or unconscious self, but her faith told her that God was speaking to her through the gift from her preconscious or unconscious self. She had the reassuring sense that God would stay faithful to Joe in his ambivalence and to her in hers. But she also knew that she was being invited to stay connected to her own deep desire to teach in a new way, not as a transmitter of truth to others but as one who creates, or has a principal role in creating, a containing environment for students and herself. That environment might eventually lead to transformative learning in ways tailored to the student and ways that only the student could name. Lecturing, input, would be one of her activities, but the larger one would be the exercise of authority as container of environment for the group's lurching, conflicted, but also promising work of learning about that elusive but crucial human value, the common good.

At the beginning of the next class Alice felt committed to holding steady with Joe and with others whose expectations she was frustrating. She did not feel isolated, even though at the moment she was not working with a human partner. She gave the lecture part but then encouraged the class members to work with each other and not just with her, as the authority in the class. It came to her, as well, that she needed a human partner to process what was happening to her and the class. She asked a fellow teacher to sit down with her once a week so that she could process the "buttons" that were pushed in her in the class and her manner of responding to the class's dynamics.

At the end of the course the student evaluations were mixed. Some thought that the wall between classroom and real world had been breached in a way that allowed useful learning under pressure to occur. Others were just as firm that the unsafety in the class was too much for learning to go on. For her part, Alice felt a commitment to stay with this style of teaching and to continue to learn how to do it better.

The Source of My Identity

Second, the person in authority needs to have a sense of personal identity that allows her to disidentify from the projections that are sent her way by members of the group. Disidentification is a psychological skill that permits one to distance oneself in a healthy way from the negative messages sent in one's direction. But spirituality offers a deeper resource. The person in authority who is a person of faith can grow as someone who exists in the sight of God, whose authentic identity comes from God and for that very reason belongs to the individual. Here gift and autonomy are not in opposition.

The more something comes to us from God the more it is truly ours.

To grow in the conviction that I am someone who exists here and now because, here and now, I am being created by the infinite care and love of someone whose entire being is one act of love of me (to the exclusion of no other), is to touch into the mysterious depth that underlies human narcissism. We are infinitely fascinated by ourselves. We believe we are unique, special, and of unlimited lovableness. (On some other levels, of course, we know that we can doubt this as well.) But the Christian understanding of the roots of narcissism grounds that endless self-fascination in God's infinite love for me, which *creates* my being and my lovableness. The secret is that I need constantly to receive that being, lovableness, and specialness as pure gift, not as achievement. I skew my existence when I turn what is lastingly a gift into a possession or achievement of my own.[11]

As a person in authority I can remain more faithful to my role for the common good of the group if I can locate the root of my identity, and that of members in the group, in the creative action of God in my life and in theirs.

When Mark assumed the position of project director in his software company, he knew a lot would be riding on his shoulders. The project's outcome could spell either a new future for the firm or its last gasp as a small entrepreneurial outfit. He was spending more and more time on the project—the development of an innovative software package for the entertainment business. His boss was constantly looking over his shoulder, communicating his own anxiety to Mark. Both his boss and some of his associates were getting the message across to him that the success of this project would guarantee Mark's future. (The implicit underside of this, of course, was that, if he failed, he would become a nobody.) Mark began to lose sleep, his communication with his wife was shriveling up, and he was spending zero time with his daughter.

Occasionally he would think of the irony of his situation. Here he was trying to come up with a product that would help the entertainment business, and he was getting eaten alive by his involvement in developing the project. As the weeks went on, and he solved a technical problem or helped one of his subordinates tackle a problem on another part of the project, he began to lose his bearings. The other team members seemed to be putting onto him, the director, all manner of expectations about the success of the project. As he solved elements that proved intractable to others, their expectations only increased. Whenever he attempted to return to others the work that belonged properly in their hands, he found himself on the receiving end of an enormous amount of heat. One day an associate very angrily accused him of shirking his responsibility and "loading it on us." He tried not to take this personally, but that was hard to do. It all seemed aimed at him. How was he *not* to take it personally?

On a rare evening at home with his family, Mark recalled something he had learned from one of his brothers, who had taken a course in psychosynthesis. His brother had loaned him a book that talked about the fact that the human person is populated by many parts or roles, which are *of* the person, but that the person is more than those parts or the sum of them. Knowing this, the person could move gradually away from this portion or that role, consciously "disidentifying" from that role or part, and align with that self who has the roles but is not exhaustively identical with any of them. He reread the chapter that dealt with this question, and tried to use the technique that it described.[12]

At work the next day, Mark tried to remember the insight of the previous evening. He recalled that he was more than what his associate said to him, that he was in fact more than this job, important as it was. He brought to mind the relationships that were most important to him—his relationship with his wife and child, and deeper than that, his relationship to what he called his "Source," the One in whose presence he lived, breathed, and worked. He found that, for the present, he was able to continue to stay at the task without it eating him up. He hoped that he could hold that vision and not fall into letting his identity be handed over to the project. He knew he would need to be alert.

Over the ensuing weeks, Mark found that he worked for days at a time without a healthy "disidentification" from the project, and that when he did so, his subordinates would project increasingly oppressive expectations onto him. It seemed to him that he needed some regular meditation time each day, but how could he fit it into his already hopeless schedule?

After a while he decided he simply had to make meditation a priority. He decided to spend twenty minutes each day in quiet. He would sit down, place himself in the presence of God, and then ask God to stay with him while he "sat with" different portions of himself, as though they were persons with whom he could communicate. Mark first "sat with" his frustrated self, and asked it how it felt, and then listened. At first this felt very odd, but he asked God to help with this. Soon he sensed that he was being addressed by his frustrated self, who seemed to be all bent out of shape, dying to be listened to. As he listened, he sensed God listening too, and in that welcoming space, the frustration found a voice. As the weeks went on, other parts of himself spoke out: his angry self, his ambitious self, his self as pleaser, and his self as yearning for contact with God, in and through the tough stuff.

The effect on his day was palpable. Mark soon found the courage to claim his superiors' attention and ask that a review of responsibilities be initiated, with the goal of reapportioning assignments in a healthier way. The part of himself that needed to please was not dead and gone, but it had yielded for now, at least, to a more forthright and honest self in relation to authority figures.

The Life of the Group

A person in authority needs to grow in the ability to interpret the group's life as more than the sum of the individual members. Theorists of organizational life generally maintain that the life of the group as a whole has identifiable features, and these features are lived out by members or subgroups within the group. Two of the most basic dynamisms in human beings are the drive to belong to something larger than oneself and the drive to become oneself (to be a part, and to be apart). From the perspective of faith and in attunement with Ignatian spirituality, it is possible to provide the holding environment for the group with the conviction that God has desires for the well-being of the group. The deepest and most authentic longings of the members of the group are expressive in a finite, human way of God's longing for the flourishing of humanity.

Cultivating a sense of reverence for the life of the group is one way of staying attuned to God's longings for the welfare of the group. Wonder at the fact that people come together in quest of a reality larger than themselves, that they place their sense of autonomy at risk to some degree by entering the group, can help the person in authority avoid developing a manipulative relationship with the group. In a situation of transformational work there is a great deal of disequilibrium and people can have many buttons pushed. If the authority person can find ways of appealing to the deeper longings of the members of the group, it can help to return the work that is properly the group's back to the group, when the members may well want to put the responsibility of coming up with the answer to the transformational challenges squarely on the shoulders of the authority person.

Professions are supposed to be forms of work that

are rooted in a spirit of service, of commitment to the common good at the expense of the convenience of those involved, with standards of behavior that reflect the service dimension of the work. Very often people enter a profession—as educator, physician, or lawyer, for example—out of a desire to contribute to the well-being of others. It is apparent to most nowadays that it is increasingly difficult to remain connected to that deep sense of purpose as one prepares to enter an increasingly specialized profession and tries to respond to the financial debts incurred during his or her education.

When Sally came back from the weekend retreat with her Legal Aid team, she realized that the temptation would once again be powerful to return to a bureaucratic way of handling the case load. The three-day retreat had helped her recognize how affected she and her twelve-person staff had been by the sheer volume of work. With the help of a centered and perceptive outside consultant, the weekend had had the desired effect of bringing her back to center and reminding her of the basic reason why she had become a lawyer in the first place. One of her teachers in college had profoundly affected her with his conviction that some moral values, such as civil rights, could become incarnate in good laws, even at times outpacing some people's personal moral convictions. Changing structures can help change people's consciousness, was one way he expressed it. This same teacher had maintained that the deepest law at work in the universe was the law of love and truth, and that, if one allied oneself with that

157

fundamental law, one's efforts to better the condition of people would be aligned with the deepest grain of the universe.

For Sally that law was not an impersonal entity, but she found it very difficult to sense the presence and activity of that loving and truthful One in the cluttered, chaotic space of her incredibly busy office. As she drove back from the retreat, alone in her car, she savored an image that emerged spontaneously on the last night of retreat: an image of her team of lawyers as a living, pulsing body, with each individual a member of the body, contributing something unique to the whole.[13] And she sensed that that body was somehow an incarnation of that mystery of love and truth with which she sought to cooperate in her professional work. She resolved to let herself savor this image for a few precious moments each workday.

Sally chose to give five minutes of her lunch hour to staying with the image of her Legal Aid team as a living organism, of which each person was a living member. This discipline paid off in concrete, if subtle, dividends. She began asking God for a sense of what the labors of her team and herself meant to God; at times she was given a sense that the team was, as she put it, "the hands of God's compassion." This sense enabled her to continue in the fray.

She also found herself asking other members of the team how they perceived the team as a whole. In fact, after doing this for a while, she found that when things would get very rushed and tense among them, they would start joking about the need to "return to the whole." This expression meant that they needed to take some time out, however briefly, to remind themselves that they were more than the sum of their parts, that their group existed to serve a larger purpose about justice, even if not all the team members would express the purpose in the religious terms used by Sally. They found even these brief "returns to the whole" refreshing. The effect was hard to describe in detail, but they seemed to help keep the team from simply turning into functionaries hell bent for burnout.

God wants to act in, through, and with groups of human beings, provided they are intent on the flourishing of human beings and not on their harm or destruction. Partnering with God, finding one's deepest identity in one's relationship with God, and developing a sense of God's longing to act in and with groups can help a person in the role of authority stay in the fray for the long haul.

Notes

1. I am indebted to Ronald Heifetz, M.D., of Harvard University's John F. Kennedy School of Government, for the images of "dance floor" and "balcony." For a brief exploration of Heifetz's theory of leadership and authority, see his essay "Political Leadership: Managing the Public's Problem Solving," in *The Power of Public Ideas,* ed. R. B. Reich (Cambridge, Mass.: Harvard University Press, 1985), 179–203.

2. Truth and love need to be discerned, of course, for

we settle too often for their illusory substitutes. The authentic versions are discovered only through healthy self-transcendence, and not by a narrow pursuit of self-satisfaction. Healthy self-transcendence entails intellectual and moral conversion as ongoing processes in our lives. See T. Dunne, *Lonergan and Spirituality: Towards a Spiritual Integration* (Chicago: Loyola University Press, 1985).

3. For an exploration of this fundamental ambivalence with regard to group life, see K. K. Smith and D. N. Berg, *Paradoxes of Group Life: Understanding Conflict, Paralysis, and Movement in Group Dynamics* (San Francisco: Jossey-Bass, 1990).

4. Dunne, *Lonergan and Spirituality,* 119. I am indebted to Tad Dunne for this treatment of what are classically known as the three theological virtues.

5. Dunne, *Lonergan and Spirituality,* 123.

6. Dunne, *Lonergan and Spirituality,* 125.

7. G. P. Gauss, *The Spiritual Exercises of Ignatius of Loyola: A Translation and Commentary* (St. Louis: Institute of Jesuit Sources, 1992).

8. Very helpful as an orientation to Ignatian spirituality is David Lonsdale's *Eyes to See, Ears to Hear: An Introduction to Ignatian Spirituality* (Chicago: Loyola University Press, 1990).

9. Gauss, *The Spiritual Exercises.*

10. M. O'Sullivan, "Trust Your Feelings but Use Your Head: Discernment and the Psychology of Decision Making," *Studies in the Spirituality of Jesuits 22(4).* St. Louis: Institute of Jesuit Sources, Sept. 1990.

11. See S. Moore, *Jesus the Liberator of Desire* (New York: Crossroad, 1989). As portrayed by John Haughey in Chapter Three, Vaclav Havel is a person whose identity is fundamentally nourished by a relationship to Mystery, or to the integrity of Being. He is a marvelous example of a public figure of the late twentieth century seeking to find new language in which to speak of spirit.

12. P. Ferrucci, *What We May Be: Techniques for Psychological and Spiritual Growth Through Psychosynthesis* (Los Angeles: Tarcher, 1982), ch. 4.

13. This experience is akin to spirit as "common ground" as described by D. Susan Wisely and Elizabeth M. Lynn in Chapter Five.

7

What Leaders Cannot Do Without

The Spiritual Dimensions of Leadership

Rabindra N. Kanungo
Manuel Mendonça

At a time when impressive breakthroughs in technology are providing new and better products and services, when improved communications are transforming the world into a global village, when democracies are sprouting in former communist lands, and when the standard of well-being in Western countries seems on an ever-upward spiral, we are simultaneously witnessing events that make us question whether so much progress is indeed "progress." For example, we see reports of widespread bribery by Italian and Japanese government officials, exorbitant salaries for executives in North America, extensive environmental pollution in eastern Europe, and other instances of immoral or morally questionable conduct in our organizations. In many otherwise prosperous and affluent cities, we see an increase in the numbers of homeless people and their lengthening lines at food banks. Even those who are fortunate enough to have a job find that work is not only *not* an opportunity for growth and self-fulfillment, but a source of anxiety and insecurity. They constantly worry that their jobs may be the next sacrifice on the altar of short-term objectives in a world of quarterly profits, market share, and return on investment.

The preceding litany of woes most likely provoked the recent observation by psychologist and management consultant O. A. Ohmann: "Our people have lost faith in the basic values of our economic society, . . . we need a spiritual rebirth in industrial leadership. . . . Can it be that our *god of production* has feet of clay? Does industry need a new religion—or at least a better one than it has had?"[1] In the popular media as well as in academic journals, we see great interest in the proposition that business and other organizational leaders need to become more responsible not just to their stockholders but also to other stakeholders—consumers, employees, suppliers, government, and local communities. It is increasingly recognized that ethical principles ought to govern their decisions and that our schools ought to regard character formation as the core element of their mission. As author Clarence Walton observes: "Teachers cannot ignore what leaders cannot do without." Similar

163

sentiments are echoed by Harvard Business School professor Kenneth Andrews: "The problem of corporate ethics has three aspects: the development of the executive as a moral person; the influence of the corporation as a moral environment; and the actions needed to map a high road to economic and ethical performance—and to mount guardrails to keep corporate wayfarers on track."[2]

Put quite simply, the quality of life and perhaps the very survival of a human society depend on the moral caliber of its members. This moral caliber, however, is largely determined by people in leadership positions. The way leaders function in their positions of influence directly contributes to strengthening or weakening the moral fiber of a society. The lives of a Buddha, Mohammed, Lao-Tzu, Gandhi, and Socrates—to name a few—attest to their salutary influence in their own day as well as for all time. On the other hand, when government officials in France knowingly permit the use of contaminated blood, which results in the deaths of several hundred hemophiliacs, we see strikingly the harm that a few can inflict upon a society. When people in leadership positions compromise their moral values, they do more than physical harm. Their callous neglect or compromise of moral values also contributes to creating an atmosphere of cynicism that, like a cancer, can corrode the moral health of society.

It is in the context of the absolute need for moral leadership in organizations and in society that this chapter examines the spiritual dimensions of leadership. Specifically, we will explore the nature of spirituality and its dimensions of expression in an individual; how these same dimensions manifest themselves in leading others; and how spiritual experiences can occur for both the leader and followers when a leader engages in practices that are consistent with moral principles. Our chapter concludes with some observations on the sources identified by spiritual sages over the ages that leaders can draw upon for their spiritual strength and inspiration.

Spirituality, Its Nature and Manifestations

The Oxford dictionary defines *spiritual* as "of spirit as opposed to matter; of the soul especially as acted on by God: . . . inner nature of man." It defines *spirit* as the "intelligent or immaterial part of man, soul."[3] These meanings suggest the dual natures—spiritual and material—of human beings. Yet just as a piece of pottery is not clay in a shape but shaped clay, in the same manner, philosophical traditions that go back to Aristotle and Aquinas have always regarded a human being not as a body plus a spirit (soul) but as matter made real by a spirit (soul) resulting in a unique person. Spirituality is not something separate from the body.

As a whole person, a human being functions not just through the physical body but also through the use of the intellect and the will. Using the external senses (sight, hearing, touch, taste, smell) and internal mental processes (memory and imagination), the intellect penetrates those deep levels of reality that are in essence

165

spiritual in nature but that the physical senses and processes cannot access. It does this through abstract concepts and ideas that help to make sense of and give meaning to the objects, events, and people that one observes and experiences. The will, as expressed in a person's intention, is the power that acts in the light of intellectual knowledge. Will, as we shall see, helps us to make moral choices in living a spiritually guided life.

To develop spiritually, we need both intellect and will. In essence, we need these to overcome the pull of the sensory world, which would otherwise lead us to a self-centered and hedonistic way of living. The intellect allows us to conceive of higher values and ideals. While we tend to think of the intellect as a self-serving analytical tool, it has this other side, which enables us to ascend from the domain of the senses to the domain of ideals. It is here in the domain of ideals that spirituality resides.

Assuming the existence of a domain of ideals in human life, how do we describe the concept of spirituality and its place in that domain? If we search for its meaning in the various religions of the world, spirituality is difficult to define in a manner that is universally acceptable. Since religious beliefs and rites differ widely from age to age and from one society to another, it might be difficult to arrive at a consensus on what constitutes spirituality. However, if we analyze the spiritual experience per se and its behavioral manifestations among individuals of different religious backgrounds, it becomes evident that there is much accord on the understand-

166

ing and appreciation of the essence of spirit at three levels: cognitive, affective, and outward behavior. The commonality of spiritual experiences at each of these three levels transcends the diversity of religious practices and beliefs, and as in the material world, it can be comprehended, felt, and acted upon.

The Cognitive and Affective Levels of Spiritual Experience

At a cognitive level, spiritual experience represents a realization that, at the core of human existence, there is a set of cardinal virtues and capital vices. Ideally, the goal of human life is to live these values and overcome the vices. Virtues are the good habits that enable us to strive toward realizing our full potential. They have been traditionally identified as prudence, justice, fortitude, and temperance. Interestingly, these categories have their origin in some of our earliest philosophical thinking. For example, it was the contemporaries of Socrates who "cultivated not only the idea of virtue, which signified human rightness, but also the attempt to define it in that four-fold spectrum. This particular intellectual framework, the formula which is called the 'doctrine of virtue,' was one of the great discoveries in the history of man's self-understanding," according to the philosopher Josef Pieper.[4]

They are termed the cardinal virtues because they are the "hinges upon which a man's life swings; they are the root virtues to which all the other perfect or complete virtues can be reduced."[5] For example, consider the popular virtue of curiosity. It can give individuals the ability to acquire a high level of knowledge, to acquire competence in a specific field such as in science, in crafts, or in the arts. But its practice does not guarantee that it will be used in a just manner. There are exceptionally knowledgeable and competent individuals who become criminals or who act unjustly. By contrast, a person who practices the virtue of justice acquires the ability to act justly and, by that very fact, acts justly. Stated simply, the practice of common virtues makes a person good in one or more areas of human endeavour, but the practice of the cardinal virtues makes that person a good person.

At an affective or emotional level, the spiritual experience represents a complete trust and dependence on such virtues. In its most sublime, the spiritual experience represents a complete identification with these values or with an individual embodying these values, the aim being to achieve some form of enduring blissful state of existence. The Hindu religious tradition, as expressed in the Vedas, describes this state as sat-chit-ananda; the Christian religious tradition refers to it as attaining the beatific vision. It is a state very different from the day-to-day experiences of the self in relation to its material nature.

There is nothing mythical or unreal about these kinds of spiritual experiences. On the contrary, they can be very real. They are psychologically mediated in the sense that individuals experience spirituality when they identify with or are committed to such a set of values or to an individual symbolizing these values.[6]

Spiritual Experiences
in Our Outward Behavior

How is the spiritual experience expressed in outward behavior? What are the sources of the norms, principles, and standards of human behavior within the spiritual domain? Responses to such questions generally come from the prescriptions of moral science or ethics. The Oxford dictionary defines *moral science* or *ethics* as pertaining to the study of "moral principles, rules of conduct" and *moral* as "concerned with character or disposition, or with the distinction between right and wrong."[7] Clearly moral science or ethics goes well beyond the mere observance of the laws of the country. It is not a question of an act being legal or illegal, but whether the act is good or evil. A legal act may not necessarily be a morally good act. For example, at the Nuremburg trials all the accused had committed acts that were perfectly legal in their society but not morally good. A morally good act is necessarily an expression of a spiritual act.

According to Thomas Aquinas, a morally good act has three parts: (1) the objective act itself; (2) the subjective motive of the actor; and (3) the situation or circumstances in which the act is done. Thus, to act justly is an objectively good act, just as to murder is an objectively evil act. The individual must always have good intentions. For example, making charitable donations only to avoid paying income tax negates the moral goodness of an objectively good act. The situation or circumstances must also be considered. Giving alms to the poor is, other things being equal, a morally good act; but refusing alms to the poor person who you know would spend it on an alcoholic addiction is equally a morally good act.

Further, morally good acts are based on moral laws that are universal because they incorporate fundamental human values such as truth, goodness, beauty, courage, and justice. These values are found in all cultures, though cultures may differ with regard to the application of these values. As Boston College philosophy professor Peter Kreeft notes, "in some societies, suicide is thought to be courageous, in others it is thought to be cowardly. But no society prefers cowardice to courage. Some societies let a man have four wives, others only one, but no society says a man may simply take any woman he wants."[8]

The ability to distinguish between morally good and evil acts is critical to the formation of character. Knowing ethical principles alone (as criteria for distinguishing between good and evil acts) is of little value unless we make an effort to habitually incorporate these principles in our behavior. As Clarence Walton observes: "Character is more than what simply happens to people. It is what they do to themselves."[9] It constitutes an inner-directed and habitual strength of mind and will. The acquisition of such habitual strength, known as the practice of virtue, is greatly aided by our moral mentors who guide both by precept and example. Since practice makes perfect, it is imperative, in our formation, that much thought and care are given to what we practice.

Because the values underlying the four cardinal virtues, referred to earlier, are universally accepted, we shall briefly discuss each in the context of its importance to moral behavior. We begin with prudence.

Prudence. This virtue is practiced when we habitually assess, in the light of moral standards, the situation or issue around which a decision is required. The assessment also includes the likely favorable and unfavorable consequences of the decision for ourselves as well as for others. As a result of such assessment, we can decide to make or refrain from making a decision. In addition to the knowledge and expertise that must be brought to bear on the assessment, the prudent person will not only *not* resent that others disagree with his or her views but will actively seek such information in order to better assess the situation. In other words, prudence means objectively assessing the situation and exercising sound judgment rather than simply serving our self-interests alone.

Justice. The virtue of justice requires us to strive constantly to give others what is their due. "Due" is interpreted to mean more than their legal rights. It includes whatever others might need in order to fulfill their duties and exercise their rights as individuals—for example, the right to life, to cultural, moral, and material benefits. In an organization, it might mean exercising a sense of responsibility that balances, in a fair manner, the rights of all the stakeholders.

Fortitude. This is the courage to take great risks for an ideal that is worthwhile. A courageous person faces difficult situations and strives to act positively to

171

overcome obstacles in order to do what is good and noble. One of the underlying characteristics of fortitude is perseverance and endurance against great odds, even, if necessary, at the risk of injury to ourselves or our property. However, the objective is not to suffer the injury per se but to realize good, as guided by the prudent assessment of moral duty and dictated by the demands of justice. Harold Leavitt observed in his research on visionary leaders that "determined people try to make it happen because they believe in it, not because the odds are on their side."[10]

Temperance. Of the cardinal virtues, temperance is the only one that focuses on one's self. Such a focus can have either a selfless or a selfish orientation. As Josef Pieper explains, "Genuine self-preservation is the turning of man toward himself, with the essential stipulation, however, that in this movement he does not become fixed upon himself."[11] The practice of this virtue involves distinguishing between what is reasonable and necessary and what is self-indulgent. Although it includes the reasonable use and satisfaction of our sense appetites, it also involves the effective allocation of our time, effort, and resources. Stated differently, temperance means the exercise of self-control, which, in general, would lead us to resist the temptation to overindulge in hedonistic behaviors.

The practice of all these virtues confronts us with a struggle between two fundamental but diametrically opposed choices in every context of our lives. These choices are: should my thoughts and actions be for my benefit at the cost of others, or for the benefit of others at my cost? The values inherent in the choice of "others before myself" are universal and form part of the heritage of all cultures. To illustrate this point, we cite examples from two religious traditions and cultures—the west European and the Hindu; both have fundamentally different paths to moral behavior.

The west European religious traditions have been formed by the thinking of both the Greeks and the Romans and by Judaism and Christianity. Hinduism—or, more appropriately, the Hindu view of life—is based on religious truths that have been expounded over the millennia by the *rishiis*—the wise sages—and are contained essentially in the tales of two epics, the Ramayana and the Mahabharata. Despite these differences, we find interesting parallels in the hierarchy of values in relation to the "self or other" question. In both religious cultures, the "self or other" relationship can be considered at broadly three levels. The lowest level focuses on behaviors exclusively geared to the gratification of the self; for example, *eros* in Western traditions or *kama* in Hinduism. The next level corresponds to behaviors primarily motivated by familial considerations, helping those who are already close to you: *philia* in Western traditions or *prema* in Hinduism. The highest level consists of behaviors performed for the benefit of others, even if it comes at the cost of one's self—*agape* in Western traditions or *mokshya* in Hinduism.

To recapitulate the discussion so far, spiritual experience is not an oddity. It is of the very essence of human beings to function in the spiritual domain. To do so requires that our behavior be governed by the habitual practice of virtues. In the final analysis, the reward of the spiritual experience is that it enables each person to grow and fully realize the tremendous potential unique to that person. As Clarence Walton puts it, "Of all living creatures, only humans have the power to shape their own character, to choose between honourable and dishonourable behavior, to tell the truth or deceive, to exploit or respect others, to work hard or slack off. Each decision so shapes the person that subsequent behavior is more predictable."[12]

If a good moral character is of the essence of every human being, then with much greater reason does it become so of leaders who, in the words of Stanford management professor Harold Leavitt, by their "vision, values, and determination add soul to the organization."[13] The next section explores the nature of leadership and the spiritual experiences of both the leader and the followers when a leader engages in practices that are consistent with objective moral principles.

The Spiritual Dimensions of Leadership

On the surface of it, leadership—especially charismatic leadership—is characterized by the following features. First, it is highly relational; followers depend on their leader. Second, in this relationship, followers develop a strong emotional bond with the leader, often characterized by an abiding faith and an unwavering trust. Third, the development of such an emotional bond is triggered by the followers' experience of some crises that have affected them personally.[14]

These three characteristics of leadership are also echoed in our spiritual experiences. In almost all religions, spirituality is associated with a belief in relating oneself with a higher-order influence. The relationship is one of dependence on this superhuman or supernatural agent, manifested in different forms in different religions. For some, the agent is perceived to be another human, a guru or a saint, who embodies to a high degree all the good and noble qualities that human beings can aspire to. Some even perceive the physical presence of nature itself to be so overpowering that they develop a dependence on it with awe and wonder, as is the case when they worship the sun, fire, and other aspects of nature. For others, the agent is conceived as an abstraction in the form of God, the supreme being—omniscient, omnipotent, and omnipresent; in some religions, such an agent is an impersonal being, in others a personal being.

In this dependent spiritual relationship, followers of various religions also experience a strong emotional bond with the agent and demonstrate their unconditional trust and unquestioning faith in the agent to guide their behavior. Regardless of the form in which the agent is perceived, the followers attribute extraordinary, idealized, and visionary qualities to the agent. Furthermore, while relating to this idealized agent, it is not uncommon that the spiritual experiences among the followers of various religions, experiences such as dependence, trust, or faith, might also be triggered by the experiences of crisis in their life.

Although there is such a surface resemblance between our experiences of leadership and spirituality, this resemblance does not necessarily imply that leadership always has a spiritual dimension to it. Rather we must look more deeply at whether certain dimensions of spiritually centered leadership are present and how they affect us psychologically. For this purpose, the next few sections explore the different components of leadership that can contain or manifest a spiritual dimension. These components are the spirituality in the leadership experience, the rituals that reinforce the leader's spiritual influence, the self-identity of the leader, the leader's manner in exercising power, and the use of empowering practices.

Spirituality in the Leadership Experience

In the history of humankind, religious leaders and social reformers have continually experimented with new forms of values and ideals to improve existing conditions. For example, in Hinduism, as stated in the *Bhagavadgita,* it is believed that from time to time the world gets engulfed in vice through the acts of evil forces. God then takes human form to break this older order and eliminate vice and vindicate the virtuous, thereby establishing peace and order for humankind. Such beliefs reinforce the idea that, in the eyes of Hindu followers, spirituality guided leaders are viewed as a God figure. The followers tend to identify with these leaders and internalize their ideals and values. In the process, the relationship becomes a spiritual experience for the followers. For the leaders, their idealized values, the meaning they create for their organizations, and their commitment to realizing their vision all represent their spiritual experience. Much of the impetus for this comes from being exposed to experiences of real-world limitations, imperfections, sorrows, and suffering, as in the case of a Buddha or a Francis of Assisi. Reflections on experiences of the imperfection of the material world give rise to the spiritual experience of a more perfect and idealized world.

Spiritually guided leaders in nonreligious situations go through a similar process: from experiencing the limitations of the status quo to experiencing an idealized vision for the future that is discrepant from the status quo. The realization of an idealized vision can be a profoundly transforming spiritual experience. The essence of the experience is that spiritually guided leaders identify with a set of values that, according to political scientist James McGregor Burns, raise them to "higher levels of motivation and morality."[15] The leaders' commitment to higher levels of morality and their self-actualizing motivation to achieve their visions are often manifested in their fortitude or in the form of personal risks and sacrifices. Although risks and sacrifices by themselves do not necessarily indicate a spiritual experience, what is noteworthy is that the transforming spiritual experience resulting from the leaders' commitment to the idealized vision becomes a powerful motivational force to bear and even gladly suffer the hardships and sacrifices that may be necessary. The spiritual experience resulting from the leaders' commitment to an idealized vision is not a fleeting phenomenon. It continues to endure in the leaders through the regular performance of rituals.

Spirituality and Leadership Rituals

Organizational leaders often engage in rituals that influence their own self-image and those of their followers, much as religious leaders do. Leaders represent in essence certain ideals in their person, and rituals assist in reinforcing the link between the person and those ideals. Other rituals are performed as exercises in self-discipline. Rituals can be an important means to demonstrate spiritual intent. Through them, it is possible to strengthen one's personal commitment and internalize the idealized values professed by the leader. For instance, during and after the Indian independence movement, Mahatma Gandhi engaged in the daily ritual of operating a spinning wheel, which inspired his fellow Indians to do the same. The production of homespun thread symbolically demonstrated his belief in the economics of self-reliance and self-sufficiency and was at the same time a potent protest against colonialism as represented by the importation of British textiles. Another ritual which he engaged in periodically was fasting. The self-discipline inherent in this ascetic practice was aimed at transforming himself and served as an example of the self-restraint he expected from his followers in the path of nonviolence he advocated.

The main objective of such rituals is to bring about a self-transformation or changes in the core values held by both the leader and the followers. As psychiatrist Alan Ronald puts it, "Cognitively, rituals express the constant interchange and interpretation of the divine with the mundane."[16]

Spirituality and Self-Identity

When we analyze the self-identity of leaders who have had a transformational influence on their followers and who themselves have undergone self-transformation, it becomes apparent that they are primarily motivated by what psychologist Abraham Maslow called self-actualization needs—the highest level in his hierarchy of needs.[17] Leaders devise idealized visions that represent states of profound consciousness, identify with them, and commit themselves to achieve these visions—all of which directly contribute to realizing their potential. Thus, leaders must first undergo a self-transformation, which then serves as a model to inspire their followers to undergo a similar inner transformation. As indicated earlier in this chapter, this self-transformation at the deeper level of values is not transformation in any material sense but transformation in a spiritual sense.

Ronald's conceptualization of the self can be used here to further emphasize the point that the self-transformation of leaders has a spiritual component. He asserts that there are three types of "overarching or super-ordinate organizations of the self: the familial self, the individualized self, and the spiritual self."[18] Each individual has the potential to develop self-identity along each of these dimensions of human experience.

The individualized self is characterized by an emphasis on the self-contained competitive and individualistic "I"—a self characterized by autonomous functioning, separate, contractual, and egalitarian relationships. This is the predominant mode of identity in North American societies. The familial self is characterized by "symbiosis-reciprocity," which means a communal orientation, a sense of "we-ness," of emotional intimacy with our group members, interdependence, and reciprocal relationships. This is the predominant mode of personal identity in Eastern societies like India and Japan.[19]

The spiritual self is characterized by the realization of inner virtues and strengths, the spiritual reality or the ideals, which the self tries to attain. Ronald writes that for a person with a spiritual self-identity, "the fundamental goal of all relationships and living is the gradual self-transformation toward finer and subtler qualities and refined aspects of power in the quest for self-realization."[20] This mode of self-identity is often observed in India and Japan but is somewhat rarer in the North American context. In the highly individualistic culture of North America, the existence of this spiritual dimension of human experience is often ignored or treated as an aberration of the normal. And yet this spiritual identity is precisely what characterizes the inner psychological world views of many spiritually guided leaders. Their identification and commitment to idealized values, their efforts to develop finer and subtler qualities in themselves, their own inner self-transformation, and their missionary zeal to bring about similar transformation in others are all reflections of their spiritual identity.

Spirituality and Power

A spiritually guided leader engages in what we would call socialized rather than personalized power. Socialized power is the use of power for the service of others, whereas personalized power is expressed as power exercised purely for one's own benefit.[21] The exercise of socialized power thus implies that the leader practices the cardinal virtues and takes personal risks and makes personal sacrifices for the benefit of the followers. On the other hand, the effort to gain material wealth and status through personalized power is the product of *eros* or *kama* in the self-centered self and not of the spiritual self.

The path to the realization of the spiritual self, as prescribed in the eight beatitudes of the sermon on the Mount (Matthew 6 and 7) or in other religious scriptures, essentially involves that the individual acts simultaneously on two fronts. The individual regards the ordinary world as transitory or illusory—*maya* in the Hindu tradition—and therefore develops an emotional detachment from it. At the same time, the individual develops a bonding with the spiritual reality that is unchanging and endures. Emotional detachment allows the leader to develop prudence and a proper perspective on the purpose and role of people, things, and events. The bonding with a spiritual reality that results from the leader's commitment to the higher purpose, and the emotional detachment from the everyday reality, enable the leader to overcome personal vices and to cope with sorrows and sufferings.

Furthermore, the leader views these events as a rich source of inner strength and insights of the human condition that are essential if the leader is to adopt the needed compassion for and an understanding of the followers. As Ronald says, "As the person becomes increasingly involved in the realization of the spiritual self, he or she still relates to others and fulfills responsibilities, but without the intense looking to the other for the fulfillment of wishes, esteem and the desire to be needed."[22] In other words, the need for socialized power and the outward behaviors to fulfill such a need through personal sacrifices reflect the increased involvement in the spiritual self.

Spirituality and Empowerment

The influence of spiritually centered leaders on their followers is more often characterized as transformational rather than transactional. The followers achieve self-transformation not through transactions in exchange for valued resources but through emotional bonding, identification with the leader, and the internalization of the idealized vision advocated by the leader. The primary objective of bringing about self-transformation in the followers is to enable them to achieve an inner strength or a set of beliefs about their capability to pursue and realize the vision.

In influencing followers to achieve inner strength and capability, the actions of spiritually guided leaders are designed to empower the followers. As Jay Conger and Rabindra Kanungo suggest, empowerment is a process of enabling or strengthening the self-efficacy beliefs (an "I can do" attitude) among followers.[23] Followers are empowered when they view the leader as an ideal model. They develop an intense emotional bond, based on trust and faith, that assures them of continued encouragement and support rather than rejection in the event of possible failures.

Being empowered by a leader who is strong and virtuous, trustworthy and supportive, is a spiritual experience. The followers' dependence on such an individual does not imply a mindless, docile, or parasitic subordination. It rather implies a dependence that allows followers to draw inspiration from the leader in order that they might be self-efficacious and, like the leader, achieve a similar self-transformation. Dependence does not result from fear of rejection or other forms of threats. Instead, spiritually guided leaders lead by personal examples of virtuous acts and by the ideals of their visions, the attraction of which is greatly enhanced by the inspiring manner in which it is described. The followers are therefore inspired to follow the leader's example, and they do so with complete autonomy

183

and by their own volition. They choose to be dependent on the leader because they are convinced that the path they follow will eventually lead to the realization of their own deepest hopes and aspirations.

The nature of this dependence is similar to that of a serious student who trustingly follows the guidance and direction of a teacher in order to grow and develop. Such dependence is best exemplified by the *chela-guru* (student-teacher) relationship in Hindu asceticism. In this relationship, the guru is revered and almost worshipped as a godhead. Through this reverence and worship, students seek the guru's blessings so that they might attain the level of knowledge, wisdom, and spiritual development of the guru. In fact, a common prayer for such blessings is "Oh Lord, through your grace the mute speaks and the lame conquers the mountain. I pray thee for your grace." The prayer obviously has a spiritual connotation; the student seeks to be empowered. The empowering experience that underlies this relationship has a strong spiritual element that substantially affects and forms the student's spiritual life. In much the same way, the follower depends on a leader for self-transformation.

In conclusion, although leadership can take various forms, such as participative or charismatic or transformational leadership, it is only when leadership takes on a more truly transformational form that the spiritual dimension comes to the fore. In other leadership roles, the leader neither pursues an idealized vision nor attempts self-transformation. The identity of such leaders can be characterized in terms of an emphasis on either individualized "I-ness" (task-oriented leadership role) or familial "we-ness" (people- and participative-oriented leadership roles). The presence of the spiritual self is most noticeable when leaders seek to transform themselves and their followers to a higher order. Cognitively, the spiritual dimension of the self is expressed in the sense of the profound consciousness of the eternal values of truth, beauty, and goodness represented by the vision of the leader. At an affective level, spirituality is manifested in the emotional bonding with the leader and in the trust and faith in the values of the leader's vision. In terms of outward behavior, spirituality radiates through symbolic rituals supported by the leader's virtuous life, which places the interest and concerns of others before self, despite the personal risks and sacrifices that may be, and in fact are, inevitably involved.

The Sources of Spiritual Strength

A leader is best when people barel;
    know that he exists.
Not so good when people obey and
    acclaim him.
Worse when they despise him.
If you fail to honour people,
    they fail to honour you;
But of a good leader,
    who talks little,
    when his work is done,
    his aim fulfilled,
    they will all say "We did this ourselves."[24]

Lao-Tzu's description of a leader aptly and succinctly makes the point that the leader's life is best epitomized by the dictum "Others before self"—at all times and regardless of the cost to self. Clearly, a leader needs great spiritual stamina to meet the challenging demands of this formidable role. This final section will explore some of the sources that leaders might draw upon to develop a moral character possessed of inner strength and resourcefulness and to develop the moral environment of their organization.

The Development of the Leader as a Moral Person

As discussed earlier, leadership has a spiritual dimension when it is transformational in nature for the leader and the followers. Such transformation must begin, however, with the leader. In the field of ethical management, authors Kenneth Blanchard and Norman Vincent Peale offer us five inspiring and practical principles for ethical power: purpose, pride, patience, persistence, perspective.[25] We will briefly discuss these principles as sources of ethical power that leaders can tap as they go about their task of self-transformation. And while the field of management has treated ethics as something separate from spirituality, we feel that, quite to the contrary, ethics is an integral part of spirituality.

Purpose. Spiritually guided leaders will find a purpose that is visionary and uplifting and will take special initiatives to achieve their vision. These initiatives might include personal sacrifice, building trust among followers, and using behavior that arouses followers' attention.[26] Leaders often exercise their ethical power by subjecting the vision as well as the means to achieve it to rigorous scrutiny in the light of the purpose that is intended to be served. What higher purpose does the vision serve? In the context of a business organization, it is universally admitted that the business must be profitable. But to what purpose? Are profits a means or an end? University of Southern California management professor James O'Toole responds that corporations committed to a higher purpose "exist to provide society with the goods and services it needs, to provide employment, and to create a surplus of wealth (profit) with which to improve the general standard of living and quality of life."[27]

The scrutiny of the vision in the perspective of its higher purpose will cause leaders to practice primarily the virtues of prudence and justice. Furthermore, the habit of questioning the purpose of one's actions in the light of ethical principles demonstrates the strength of the leaders' character, which in turn enhances their trustworthiness.

Pride. Leaders obviously need high self-esteem but this self-esteem must originate from a healthy pride in their accomplishments as well as the esteem of their followers. The dividing line between healthy pride and vanity is unbelievably thin because of a strong egoistic tendency in human beings. But spiritually guided leaders recognize that inordinate self-love is a human vice and not a virtue. However, leaders' actions must not be designed to merely gain the acceptance of the followers. For example, in formulating a vision, leaders must take into account the needs and aspirations of the followers, but at the same time must not be swayed by the desire simply to be accepted or liked by them. This might otherwise result in compromising the vision, and such compromise might jeopardize its higher purpose. In other words, leaders do not look to the followers for affiliative assurance to reinforce their sense of self-love, but rather seek to transform their followers to accept and realize the vision.[28]

Patience. As leaders work toward the realization of the vision, they are certain to come across obstacles within the environment or in the followers' reluctance to invest significant efforts and to patiently await the realization of the vision. It takes time to develop the necessary trust of the followers; leaders must possess and exhibit great patience.

There are two aspects to this faith. The first aspect is the leaders' strong beliefs in the truth and value of the higher purpose and in their vision of the future as the best way to serve that higher purpose. The second aspect relates to the strength of the leaders' conviction in spiritual beliefs. When leaders believe in a higher purpose or a Being representing the higher purpose, they develop an inner realization that "in good time" the difficulties will be resolved. The faith referred to here is not a fatalism that inevitably paralyzes action. Rather, both aspects of faith—the vision and the spiritual convictions—contribute to leaders' constancy of purpose, which leads them to continue undaunted with what needs to be done with the unshaken belief that the present difficulties are part of the progress toward realizing the vision.

This particularly will be the case with leaders who strive to exercise prudence and fortitude. As discussed in the first section, the practice of prudence enables us to properly assess all the facts and circumstances surrounding our decisions. The practice of fortitude, on the other hand, develops the capacity to act positively in the midst of difficulties. In other words, the relevance of prudence is reflected in the leaders' need to be sensitive to the environment while the relevance of fortitude is demonstrated by having to perform actions that involve great personal risks and sacrifices. Patient leaders who practice prudence and fortitude will not be inclined to resort to unethical practices when things do not go as planned.

Persistence. The power of persistence is best captured in Winston Churchill's bulldog perseverance and in one of his favorite sayings: "Never! Never! Never! Never Give Up!" Persistence does not mean a stubborn obstinacy. Rather, spiritually guided leaders will not allow difficulties to weaken their resolve to "stay the course"; instead, they continue to take the steps necessary, even those involving personal risk and sacrifice, in order to achieve the vision. It is perfectly human to take an unethical path when we feel overwhelmed by insurmountable internal or external difficulties. The practice of fortitude allows us to face difficulties not because it is convenient or pleasant to do so but because our duty requires that it be done.

In a society in which both individuals and organizations are obsessed with and guided by short-term gratification, the practice of patience and persistence becomes a real challenge. In his *Spiritual Exercises,* Ignatius of Loyola proposes that in situations where we are inclined to justify the neglect of our duty with endless rationalizations, then we are advised not to debate these rationalizations but to simply make the extra effort to do what our duty dictates.[29]

Perspective. Blanchard and Peale describe perspective as "the capacity to see what is *really* important in any given situation."[30] The habit of reflection is critical to acquiring a sense of perspective. And reflection is simply not possible unless some time each day is devoted to silence—a resource that has been recommended by wise men of all time and from all cultures, and yet one resource that remains mostly untapped. As Peter Kreeft puts it, "If I were a doctor and I could prescribe just one remedy for all the ills of the modern world, I would prescribe silence. For even if the word of God were proclaimed in the modern world, no one would hear it, because of the panoply of noise. Therefore, *create silence.*"[31]

Silence is more than refraining from noise; it is the inner silence that allows us to reflect on the higher purpose, to question our decisions in the light of that purpose, and to seek strength not to betray it. It allows us to listen to the inner stirrings of the spirit. It is critical for making distinctions—between right and wrong, to discern what we ought to do. In a parable from Kenneth Blanchard and Norman Vincent Peale's *The Power of Ethical Management,* the mentor of a manager facing an ethical dilemma comments: "I am continually amazed at how clear my thinking becomes afterward, particularly if I'm faced with a big problem. It's as if the answer I am seeking exists somewhere already, just waiting for me to tune in to it. The solitude, quiet, and reflection are the tuning-in process."[32]

The preceding discussion has touched on several suggestions available to leaders in their efforts to develop the inner strength they need to function as ethical, moral people. The enduring effectiveness of these suggestions depends upon their habitual practice and, more important, on setting aside a specific time for the practice of examining one's conscience. Few would deny that people do not suddenly find themselves engaging in grave and serious unethical practices. On the contrary, these practices are preceded by minor unethical lapses that we rationalize as either inconsequential or commonplace—"everyone else is doing it." The periodic examination of conscience prevents unethical behavior—or at least alerts us to the fact that we might be treading on its slippery slope.

The Development of a Moral Environment

The chairman of Matushita Electric was asked to define his primary job. This was his response: "To model love. I am the *soul* of this company. It is through me that our organization's values pass."[33]

The statements of the organization's vision, mission, and policies—however numerous, well-crafted, and eloquently articulated—are futile if the leader's actions and behavior are inconsistent with these statements. Actions speak louder than words; what the leader does and values set the ethical tone and create the moral environment of the organization. In 1988 key business leaders, deans of business schools, and members of Congress were asked about ethical standards and behavior; the survey report indicated that "73 percent recognize the CEO's ability to influence ethical behavior."[34]

Truly, the leader is the soul of the organization. Even in the relatively trivial area of employees' work attendance, the CEO's example has been found to be critical. However, there are other more telling examples. One manufacturer continued to produce a product known to cause illness and death. In contrast, after the Tylenol poisonings Johnson & Johnson immediately withdrew the product from its market, at enormous costs, even though the remaining capsules were completely safe.[35] The actions of these CEOs sent clear, unambiguous messages about the ethical standards expected from their employees.

The higher purpose established for an organization by its leader becomes the starting point in creating the moral environment. The higher purpose and the values it represents convey to employees what is acceptable and unacceptable behavior. To facilitate employees' internalizing such important values, a leader must develop specific codes of conduct for organizational members. These codes of conduct can be useful and even necessary, but care needs to be taken in their development.

For instance, in a survey on the codes of more than two hundred companies, the "most ignored item was personal character—it seemed not to matter."[36] In addition to codes of conduct, the leader must identify areas and issues that might be particularly susceptible to unethical conduct and must develop internal policies and processes that specifically deal with them.

The leader must also create opportunities for employees to exchange ideas and experiences in implementing a code of conduct and must be ready to help them face the difficulties they might likely encounter in acting ethically in certain situations. For example, some organizations hold periodic retreats or discussion forums that provide employees with the intellectual, emotional, and moral support necessary to maintain the high ethical standards expected of them.

Codes of conduct, related policies and procedures, and support structures are undoubtedly essential to the development of the organization's moral environment. However, in the final analysis, it is the leader's personal conduct that determines the effectiveness of the codes, policies and procedures, and the support structures. A moral environment cannot be created by the fiat of the leader. Just as Mother Teresa's work for the "poorest of the poor" is an external outpouring of her love for God, in much the same way the organization's moral environment is a natural overflow of the spiritually guided leader's commitment to ethical principles and values that are expressed not only in terms of intellectual assent but also in a daily struggle to live by them.

Ohmann cites the example of an executive whose

policies and practices flowed naturally from his beliefs and values. This executive believed that his talent and resources were gifts entrusted to his stewardship for the "maximum self-development and useful service to one's fellows in the hope that one may live a rich life and be a credit to his Creator . . . it is against this frame of reference that the decisions of the moment easily fall into proper perspective."[37] As a result, he provided employees with opportunities to develop to their fullest potential. He held his employees accountable but, at the same time, coached them on to performance levels that would justify higher rewards. He viewed profits as a measure of the successful use of his employees' potential. Instead of talking about employee communication programs, he spent most of his time in the field listening to his employees. He managed conflicts not by a sense of expediency or self-concern but by reference to what best served the organization's higher purpose. His basic values not only led to consistency in his dependability and trustworthiness but also gave meaning and significance to even the routine and inconsequential activities of the workplace. The resulting moral environment truly reflected the soul of the organization and enabled its members to internalize values that provided a firm and enduring foundation for their ethical behavior.

Notes

1. O. A. Ohmann, "Skyhooks," in *Ethics in Practice: Managing the Moral Corporation,* ed. K. R. Andrews (Boston: Harvard Business School Press, 1989), 59.

2. C. C. Walton, *The Moral Manager* (Cambridge, Mass.: Ballinger, 1988), 7; K. R. Andrews, "Ethics in Practice," *Harvard Business Review* (Sept.-Oct., 1989): 99.

3. *The Concise Oxford English Dictionary of Current English,* fifth edition (London: Oxford University Press, 1964), 1236.

4. J. Pieper, *The Four Cardinal Virtues* (New York: Harcourt, Brace and World, 1965), xi.

5. W. Farrell, *A Companion to the Summa,* vol. 3: *The Fullness of Life* (Corresponding to the Summa Theologica IIA, IIAE) (New York: Sheed & Ward, 1945), 205.

6. In Abraham Maslow's theory of meta-motivation, the spiritual experiences of pursuing values such as truth, goodness, and beauty are regarded as a major part of one's self-actualization. There is a remarkable parallel asserting these same values in Hinduism: truth (*satyam*), goodness (*sivam*), and beauty (*sundaram*). (See for example S. Radhakrishnan, *The Hindu View of Life* [New York: Macmillan, 1962].) Mortimer Adler in *Six Great Ideas* (New York: Macmillan, 1981), 24, emphasized the fact that when we think of truth, goodness, and beauty, we are thinking about the world in which we live, "about the knowledge we have of it, the desires it arouses in us, and the admiration it elicits from us." The values underlying truth, goodness, and beauty are so transcendent and universal that these ideas also become the touchstone by which we judge our outward behavior, as discussed in the next section.

195

7. *The Concise Oxford English Dictionary,* 145, 784.
8. P. Kreeft, *Making Choices: Practical Wisdom for Everyday Moral Decisions* (Ann Arbor, Mich.: Servant Publications, 1990), 34.
9. Walton, *Moral Manager,* 175.
10. H. Leavitt, *Corporate Pathfinders* (Homewood, Ill.: Dow Jones-Irwin, 1986), 95. Also see Pieper, *Four Cardinal Virtues.*
11. Pieper, J. *Four Cardinal Virtues,* 148.
12. Walton, *Moral Manager,* 176.
13. Leavitt, *Corporate Pathfinders,* 222–223.
14. See J. A. Conger and R. N. Kanungo, "Toward a Behavioral Theory of Charismatic Leadership in Organizational Settings," *Academy of Management Review, 12* (1987): 637–647.
15. J. M. Burns, *Leadership* (New York: Harper & Row, 1978), 20.
16. A. Ronald, *In Search of Self in India and Japan* (Princeton, N.J.: Princeton University Press, 1988).
17. A. H. Maslow, *Motivation and Personality* (New York: Harper & Row, 1954).
18. Ronald, *In Search of Self,* 6.
19. The individualized and the familial selves are similar to the constructs of individualism-collectivism suggested by G. Hofstede in *Culture's Consequences: International Differences in Work-Related Values* (Beverly Hills, Calif.: Sage, 1980) and H. C. Triandis in "Collectivism and Development," in *Social Values and Development: An Asian Perspective,* ed.

D. Sinha and H.S.R. Kao (New Delhi: Sage, 1988), 285–303.

20. Ronald, *In Search of Self*, 294.

21. D. C. McClelland, *Human Motivation* (Glenview, Ill.: Scott Foresman, 1985).

22. Ronald, *In Search of Self*, 307.

23. J. A. Conger and R. N. Kanungo, "The Empowerment Process: Integrating Theory and Practice," *The Academy of Management Review*, *13*(3) (1988): 471–482.

24. W. Bynner, *The Way of Life According to Lao Tzu* (New York: Capricorn Books, 1962), 34–35.

25. K. Blanchard and N. V. Peale, *The Power of Ethical Management* (New York: Fawcett Crest, 1988).

26. Conger and Kanungo, "Toward a Behavioral Theory."

27. J. O'Toole, *Vanguard Management: Redesigning the Corporate Future* (New York: Doubleday, 1985), 49.

28. R. E. Boyatzis, "The Need for Close Relationships and the Manager's Job," in *Organizational Psychology: A Book of Readings*, ed. D. A. Kolb, I. M. Rubin, and J. M. McIntyre (Englewood Cliffs, N.J.: Prentice-Hall, 1974).

29. *The Spiritual Exercises of St. Ignatius Loyola (A New Translation by Elisabeth Meier Tetlon)* (Lanham, Md.: University Press of America, 1987).

30. Blanchard and Peale, *Power of Ethical Management*, 69.

31. Kreeft, *Making Choices,* 168.

32. Blanchard and Peale, *Power of Ethical Management,* 76.

33. Blanchard and Peale, *Power of Ethical Management,* 89.

34. E. A. Kangas, "Introduction," *Ethics in American Business: A Special Report* (New York: Touche Ross, 1988), 11.

35. A. G. Lank, "The Ethical Criterion in Business Decision-Making: Optional or Imperative," *Ethics in American Business: A Special Report* (New York: Touche Ross, 1988), 47.

36. Walton, *Moral Manager,* 170.

37. Ohmann, "Skyhooks," 66–67.

8

Conclusion
Reuniting
Spirituality and Work

Jay A. Conger

*T*he purpose of this book has been to spark some small fires of possibilities—not to provide definite answers but to raise questions, to challenge and push us into thinking more deeply about the ways spirituality might play a role in workplace life and in its leadership. Many of the ideas in this book represent an entirely new way of looking at leadership. Will those ideas germinate and take hold in our workplace? In this concluding chapter I look at the prospects for successful germination, and then close with an ancient folktale that highlights some of the book's themes.

Possibilities and Obstacles

When we articulated the original vision for this book, we sensed that we had to connect spirituality to the practicing world of managers, consultants, and educators if we were to be helpful. So the approaches described in Chapters Four through Seven are all applicable to real workplaces. Some of them are quite ancient, others more recent innovations. Some are more personal, others more organizational. But most of them have a practical orientation. Our aim was to sow some very pragmatic seeds into workplace life, not just philosophical ones. In doing so, we had hoped to reach more broadly and with greater usefulness. In addition, we wanted readers to realize the magnitude of the challenge that awaits the book's ideas and practices—challenges well described in Chapters Two, Three, and Four.

Given these objectives, I often wondered as our project progressed what type of terrain these ideas and insights would be falling on. How receptive would North American workplaces actually be? Friends working as human resources managers, consultants, and executives had talked about a growing interest in the role of spirituality in work, but how broad was their perspective? So I did a survey of what has appeared in the business press on religion and work in recent years to gauge the sentiment at large in our society. From that research, I discovered several fascinating facts that have convinced me that the soil on which this book falls may indeed be quite fertile though not free of rocky places and obstacles.

For example, I relearned that America is a very religious society. Our religious life is an essential part of our character. Though a far smaller percentage are loyal churchgoers, the vast majority of Americans identify themselves as religious. While the book was underway, a major religious survey of 113,000 Americans by Dr. Martin Marty, a religion professor at the University of Chicago, was completed. From its results, Dr. Marty concluded that it was "astonishing that in a high-tech, highly affluent nation, we have *ninety* percent who identify themselves as religious. If such a poll were done in western Europe, the ancestral home of many Americans, you would run at least a third or more lower on every indicator."[1] Religion, as it turns out, is more important in America than in the majority of industrialized nations.

While religion and spirituality are not always one and the same, as I mentioned in Chapter One, it would appear that we are by nature a fairly spiritual people. This is very apparent in the many not-for-profit organizations that are guided by spiritual principles, such as the YMCA, the Salvation Army, or Alcoholics Anonymous. The person in the office next to you at work is just as likely to be religious as the person sitting by you at the temple or church.

In addition, certain denominations and faiths see spirituality as an integral part of workplace life. For example, in my research I came across several newspaper articles on the evangelical movement and its influence on the world of business. On the more humorous side, there was a story about the "Born Again Carpet Care—Carpet Cleaners Who Care." When owner Wendy Ellis was asked by a *Los Angeles Times* reporter just what the company name meant, she said: "It connotes being a Christian company. But you can take it two ways: Your carpet can be born again after being cleaned." There is even a Christian Yellow Pages. And Mike Yaconelli, editor of *The Door,* a tongue-in-cheek evangelical magazine based in San Diego, has found these ads in newspapers: "Jesus Saves Oil Changes" for a Midwest tire shop, a "Christ-healing" piano tuner, and a Dallas restaurant calling itself a "restaurant for the righteous" offering a "complete menu of pure food inspired by the Holy Spirit and Bible Food."[2]

There are also major companies run by leaders who actively espouse their spiritual values in the hopes that they will guide company behavior. The head of Mary Kay Cosmetics attributes her company's success directly to God: "We succeeded with a foundation built upon the Golden Rule and a philosophy of God first, family second, and career third, giving women a chance to keep their lives in the proper perspective." ServiceMaster, a more than $1 billion company that manages services ranging from food preparation to housekeeping to equipment maintenance for institutions, even has religious meaning in its name—"Service to the Master." Its ultimate goal is "to honor God in all we do."[3] Tom Chappell, Harvard Divinity graduate and cofounder of Tom's of Maine, a natural toothpaste and soap company, says, "The purpose of business is more than making money. . . . The CEO's of the future will be those who manage through shared values rather than directives of fear."[4] Chick-fil-A, an Atlanta-based fast-food company, holds a regular Monday morning religious service with gospel music, public prayers, and slide shows on evangelical missions around the globe.[5]

A surprising number of senior executives at Fortune 500 companies are actively religious. In a recent survey of a hundred business executives, 65 percent said they worshipped at churches or synagogues on a regular basis. This compares to a national average of 40 percent for all Americans. And the reasons why today's executives worship appear to be quite different from those of several decades ago when one went to see and be seen. A summary of the survey described today's business leaders as "under stress and seeking meaning, inspiration, and guidance for their lives. Many also welcome the ethical forums that synagogues and churches provide."[6]

Most of these executives consider religion largely a personal matter, and to be publicly outspoken about their faith is seen as a misuse of their authority and power. "Besides, it's hard enough to manage a real estate business without trying to manage the eternal prospects of my friends," J. McDonald Williams, managing partner of Trammell Crow Co., the nation's largest privately held real estate developer, told *Fortune* magazine.[7] What may happen instead is a more subtle influencing of company actions, especially around what constitutes ethical behavior. For example, Trammell Crow will not operate in communities where payoffs and bribes of local officials are part of doing business.

Most North American workers, however, park their spirituality at the front door of their workplaces. For them, the Mary Kays and Chick-fil-As are a little bit zany, too filled with missionary zeal, more proof that spirituality belongs in the church. In part, this reflects our long history of separating the sacred from the secular. Moreover, many of us are suspicious of leaders and organizations claiming to be acting in God's stead. Recent scandals involving evangelical leaders like Jim Bakker or Jimmy Swaggart have reinforced this view.

In addition, America has a unique dilemma. We are very diverse in our faiths. Unlike many nations where a few denominations or faiths dominate, America is characterized by a myriad of denominations from Methodist to Hasidic to Rastafarian. It is a rare workplace that reflects only one faith. Instead we might find half a dozen or more in a single company. Such diversity creates a deep-seated concern that in expressing our religious views we may somehow impinge on another's. This is further reinforced by a culture that separates church and state and that holds individual freedom as its highest value. There is also widespread feeling that spirituality is reserved for private moments and sacred spaces, certainly not a business setting. Forces such as these have kept active discussions of spirituality largely out of the office. We have a hard time even talking about such possibilities, and on those rare occasions when we do, it is usually in a disguised manner.

Finally, with the flurry of recent layoffs in both public- and private-sector jobs, this would indeed seem to be a time least receptive to the idea of a more spiritually led workplace. The critical breakdown in a shared sense of loyalty and commitment between employer and employee over the last several decades is one of the greatest impediments to realizing any of the ideas presented here.

Poor levels of workplace trust and strong societal values about individual freedom present considerable obstacles to the germination of the ideas in this book. Yet I, for one, am optimistic. I believe that the growing distinction between religion and spirituality in many people's minds will allow for new permutations of where and how spirituality is practiced. In a strange way, the decline of the formal influence of religious institutions has opened the door to finding and creating more spiritual experiences in everyday life. It is tilling the soil for many of the practices in this book. I also feel that the growing hunger for community offers new doorways for spirituality to enter and enrich our workplaces.

A Closing Story

In all spiritual traditions, parables and stories are a common means for sowing insights, ideas, and lessons about spirituality and our roles in the cosmic scheme. I thought it only fitting to close this book with one such story.[8] The tale poignantly describes the challenges we face as individuals, as employees, as leaders, in seeking to realize our own spirituality and ultimately a spirituality for our workplaces. It was also a personal favorite of Joseph Campbell, the scholar of mythology.

The tale is about realizing one's spiritual potential, an issue of great personal interest to me. When I was quite young, I had a near brush with death. That experience taught me at a very deep level the precious brevity of life and set me grappling with my own mortality at age four. So I have long wrestled with the issue of how we can achieve our fullest potential—spiritual and otherwise—given so little time and so many distractions.

In large part, though not always explicitly, this book is about that challenge—how to realize the spiritual potential that lies within us. The story I am about to tell illustrates that experience. It is an ancient tale from India. Like many tales from other places and times, it relies on images that for modern-day Western eyes seem at odds with our own traditions of spirituality. In this case, spirituality is framed around the conversion of a peaceful herbivore to a ferocious predator. It reminds me of the images of Tibetan gods. They look so menacing, but we later discover that their ferocious looks are actually protective. By being so fiercesome, they are able to scare away the evil spirits that might harm the faithful. Likewise, to see the real message that lies beneath the following story, we must put aside our cultural biases toward these seemingly contradictory images.

Once upon a time, there was a very large and very pregnant tigress who was famished. She came upon a small herd of goats and pounced on them with all her might. The little herd scattered like the wind, disappearing into the forest. The mother tiger had pounced so hard, however, that she died at the moment of impact.

But she also gave birth to her baby tiger. Now fortunately goats are very paternalistic creatures. As they wandered out of the forest, they spotted the little tiger and decided to adopt him. They taught him how to say "bah" and how to eat grass and do other goat activities. As he grew, however, it became clear that he would not become a superb specimen of goathood. As a matter of fact, the poor little guy suffered from constant indigestion. After all, he had a tiger's stomach and all that grass just did not match his digestive system. Nonetheless, he believed he was indeed a goat.

Then one day, when he was an adolescent, a big male tiger was wandering the same forest. He came upon the goat herd and pounced. Again, the goats scattered, and the male tiger found himself standing face to face with the little tiger. The big male tiger looked with disbelief and said, "What are you doing here with all these goats?" The little tiger responded with a "bah." Infuriated at this silly response, the big tiger shook the little one and exclaimed: "Can't you see? You're a tiger just like me. You're no goat!" The little tiger turned his head down and again uttered a "bah." With that, the big tiger grabbed the little guy by the scruff of his neck and carried him over to the edge of a very still pond where the water was like a mirror. The little tiger peered in. For the first time, he saw his face. It was the face of a tiger, not a goat!

The big tiger then picked him up and carried him back to his lair. There in one corner were some tender slices of fresh meat that the big tiger had picked up earlier that day. Grabbing several slices, he offered them to the little tiger, saying, "This is tiger food, try it." The little one looked mortified. "I'm a vegetarian!" he exclaimed. With that, the big tiger shoved a handful of meat into the little tiger's mouth. At first, the taste seemed strange, and he gagged. Then suddenly, the little tiger felt a wonderful sense of energy, of tigerhood, surging throughout his entire body. He stretched his small arms wide and opened his mouth, letting out his first little tiger roar.

That is where the story ends. While this particular tale lends itself to many interpretations, its original purpose was to illustrate spiritual development. It is saying that within each of us there is a great spiritual energy that lies largely dormant. There is a tiger in there somewhere. The problem is that we are so caught up in our mundane world—in our goathood—that we cannot see it. Instead, being a member of the herd is considered important. In the story, an older and wiser tiger must come along to awaken us. In real life, that tiger is often in the form of a spiritual leader and teacher or an event. He or she or it must awaken us to the spiritual being within, just as Vaclav Havel awoke Czechoslovakia to its spiritual potential.

In addition, the story seems to say that the process of getting in touch with and developing our spiritual side is neither easy nor automatic nor necessarily desirable. For example, we must first learn to reflect on ourselves. In the story, the big tiger pushes the little one to see the reflection of his true image in the pond. Part of that reflection for us also entails seeing our darker side, as Parker Palmer points out in Chapter Two. But as others have commented in this book, the process of reflecting is essential to contacting our spiritual side as well. Through prayer, meditation, and self-observation, we can see our true (or godly) side as the little tiger did. Reflection, then, is a critical first step in spiritual development. Without it, we remain caught in an external world of material distractions, of insecurities we can barely see, of short-term and self-serving needs, and of few connections to a larger universe. You may have noted that the little tiger at first balks in disbelief that he is a tiger, and initially he gags on the tiger food. Many of us are out of touch with our spiritual side or else wish to be. It takes time, guidance, courage, and effort. In a way, being a goat is easier. Goats simply graze. But with time—perhaps a great deal of time—we may come to realize that this hidden side is essential to us and to our well-being. But in realizing this, we face a major dilemma.

A passage from Peck's *The Road Less Traveled* captures this challenge that the spiritual path presents to each of us and the reason why we may gag at first:

> We (really) don't want God's responsibility. We don't want the responsibility of having to think all the time. As long as we can believe that godhood is an impossible attainment for ourselves, we don't have to worry about our spiritual growth, we don't have to push ourselves to higher and higher levels of consciousness and loving activity; we can relax

and just be human. If God's in his heaven and we're down here, and never the twain shall meet, we can let Him have all the responsibility for evolution and the directorship of the universe. . . . If we seriously listen to this "God within us," we usually find ourselves being urged to take the more difficult path, the path of more effort rather than less. To conduct the debate is to open ourselves to suffering and struggle.[9]

You might say that from the perspective of this book, the workplace is our community of goats. So immersed are we in it that we never awaken to its spiritual possibilities, nor ours. Instead, work is a place for secular rewards and challenges, and for secular leadership. There is a certain comfort and ease to it all despite, perhaps, an underlying frustration. The effort to change it would probably require that sense of responsibility that Peck is describing.

The tale of the tiger divides the world into two, just as we normally divide the sacred from the secular. Yet, for us, this division is more cultural and self-imposed than a necessary reality. It is conceivable that transformation could actually occur even within the community of goats. They do not have to be dragged off to realize their spiritual potential. Such a transformation could conceivably happen at the office. Leadership and many practices described in this book could play vital roles in that process.

There is a final aspect to the story that is essential

to spiritual development, but one that poses a dilemma to our attempts to cultivate spirituality consciously at work through a particular approach or practice. In the story, an outside event (the big tiger) must come along and awaken us to our potential. This is the gift of grace. Grace is something we have not spoken much about in this book. Yet it is clear that the little tiger did not go looking for his enlightenment. Rather, quite miraculously it came to him. Spirituality is perhaps more often a gift of grace. This poses an interesting challenge for those of us who believe that a concerted effort at anything will eventually produce results. Spirituality may prove quite to the contrary. In the Hindu faith, for example, it is said that one must follow spiritual practices but at the same time expect no gain.

Scott Peck's reflections on grace describe the problem that we must face as we wrestle with spiritual development:

I have been writing of spiritual growth as if it were an orderly, predictable process. It has been implied that spiritual growth may be learned as one might learn a field of knowledge through a Ph.D. program; if you pay your tuition and work hard enough, of course you will succeed and get your degree. . . . At the same time, I know that that's not the way it is at all. We do not come to grace; grace comes to us. Try as hard as we might to obtain grace, it may yet elude us. We may seek it not, yet it will find us. Consciously we may avidly desire the spiritual life but then discover all manner of stumbling blocks in our way. Or we may have seemingly little taste for spiritual life and yet find ourselves vigorously called to it in spite of ourselves. While on one level, we do choose whether or not to heed the call of grace, on another it seems clear that God is the one who does the choosing. The common experience of those who have achieved a state of grace . . . is one of amazement at their condition. They do not feel they have earned it."[10]

There is perhaps no answer to the issue of grace—who, why, how? I for one am at a loss in speaking to the issue, since I truly believe it is part of God's mystery. It is important, however, to understand its ultimate role in shaping our spirituality and in helping us to see that we are part of a larger Creation and that we ourselves are not the masters of this world. I do suspect, however, that the gifts of grace are not rare but widely distributed and that many of the ideas in this book are examples of such gifts.

Notes

1. "Portrait of Religion in U.S. Holds Dozens of Surprises," *New York Times* (Apr. 10, 1991): 1.
2. T. Drummond, "In God We Advertise," *Los Angeles Times* (July 29, 1991, Section E): 2.
3. E. C. Baig, "Profiting with Help from Above," *Fortune* (Apr. 27, 1987): 38.
4. M. Cox, "Business Books Emphasize the Spiritual," *Wall Street Journal* (Dec. 14, 1993): B1.

5. Baig, "Profiting," 36.
6. "God Gets Down to Business," *Across the Board,* The Conference Board 14 (5) (May 1988): 11–12.
7. Baig, "Profiting," 36–42.
8. J. Campbell, *The Power of Myth,* with Bill Moyers (Saint Paul, Minn.: HighBridge, 1988) audiotape. Also available in H. Zimmer, *Philosophies of India,* ed. J. Campbell (Cleveland, Ohio and New York: World, 1956), 4.
9. M. S. Peck, *The Road Less Traveled* (New York: Simon and Schuster, 1978), 270, 273.
10. Peck, *Road Less Traveled,* 307.

Index